A GUIDE TO
CONTROLLING YOUR
CORPORATION'S FUTURE

A GUIDE TO CONTROLLING YOUR CORPORATION'S FUTURE

RUSSELL L. ACKOFF

JAMSHID GHARAJEDAGHI

The Wharton School
University of Pennsylvania

ELSA VERGARA FINNEL

Phoebe Memorial Hospital
Albany, Georgia

JOHN WILEY & SONS

New York   Chichester   Brisbane   Toronto   Singapore

Library of Congress Cataloging in Publication Data:

Ackoff, Russell Lincoln, 1919-
   A Guide to Controlling Your Corporation's Future.
   Bibliography: p.
   Includes index.
   1. Corporate planning. I. Finnel, Elsa Vergara.
II. Gharajedaghi, Jamshid. III. Title.
HD30.28.A248 1983   658.4'012   84-14772
ISBN 0-471-88213-5

Printed in the United States of America

10 9 8 7 6 5 4 3 2 1

PREFACE

The thinking behind interactive planning and the process itself
are described in detail in *Creating the Corporate Future* (Ackoff,
1981). Then why this guide?

At the request of a corporate sponsor we prepared a guide to
facilitate use of interactive planning by units widely dispersed
around the world. Other organizations, public as well as private,
and our students found it more useful than "the original" when
trying to carry out such planning. This revision is based on re-
sponses from those who used the earlier version.

Interactive planning is applicable to any type of organization
or system, but the guide focuses on its application to corporations and those of their parts that have their own management.
Such planning can be carried out by parts of an organization
even if the organization as a whole is not so engaged. However,
the maximum benefit can be realized only when an organization as a whole and all of its parts engage in it simultaneously
and interdependently.

Planning is as much an art as it is a science. For this reason it
is impossible to specify a set of steps that guarantee attainment
of a good plan. The most that can be done is to suggest a procedure to serve as a guide, a theme on which variations should

be written to suit the unique characteristics of planners, the organization planned for, and the conditions under which the planning is done. The purpose of a guide, in contrast to that of a manual, is to stimulate choice, not to restrict it, yet at the same time to give it direction.

RUSSELL L. ACKOFF
JAMSHID GHARAJEDAGHI
ELSA VERGARA FINNEL

Philadelphia, Pennsylvania
Albany, Georgia
October 1983

CONTENTS

CHAPTER ONE

Background

■ ■ ■

ALTERNATIVE TYPES OF PLANNING

Interactive planning differs significantly from two more commonly used types of planning: *reactive* and *preactive.*

Reactive Planning

Reactive planning is bottom-up tactically oriented planning. What strategy it contains is implicit, a consequence of numerous independently made tactical decisions. It begins with the lowest or low-level units of an organization identifying the deficiencies and threats they face. Then they attempt to return to a preferred earlier state by designing projects intended to reveal the causes of these deficiencies and threats and to remove or suppress them. Next, using cost-benefit analyses, priorities are assigned to projects. Finally, using an estimate of the amount of resources that will be available for work on projects, a set of them is selected starting at the top of the priority list, working down until all the expected resources have been allocated. The set of projects thus selected constitutes the unit's plan.

Unit plans are passed up to the next higher-level unit, where they are edited and coordinated and integrated with a plan similarly prepared at that unit. This process is continued until the accumulated plans reach the top of the organization, where again they are edited, coordinated, and integrated with projects designed at that level. This, then, is the corporate plan.

Reactive planning has two major deficiencies. First, it is based on the mistaken assumption that if one gets rid of what one does not want, one gets what one wants. This assumption can be seen as false by anyone who turns on a television set and

3 ■

gets a program he or she does not want. The viewer can get rid of it by changing to another channel, but this does not necessarily result in something better.

Second, reactive planning is carried out in parts of an organization independently of other parts at the same and higher levels. An organization, however, is a system whose major deficiencies arise from the ways its parts *interact*, not from their actions taken separately. Therefore, it is possible and even likely that improvement of the performance of each part of an organization considered separately will result in a deterioration of the performance of the organization as a whole.

Preactive Planning

Preactive planning is top-down strategically oriented planning. Objectives are explicitly set but tactics are left to the discretion of individual units. Such planning has two parts, *prediction* and *preparation*, of which prediction is the more important. If a prediction is in error, even good preparation for what it predicts may be in vain.

The preactive planning process begins at the top of an organization with preparation of one or more forecasts of the future. These are analyzed for the threats and opportunities they present. Then a broad statement of overall organizational strategies for dealing with these threats and opportunities is prepared. The predicted future(s) and the strategic "white paper" are then passed down through the organization. Each level adjusts the forecast and the analysis to its own specific environmental conditions, and selects objectives and goals that are compatible with those of the organization as a whole. Programs to pursue these objectives and goals are formulated in general terms.

The accumulation of forecasts, objectives to which commitments are made, and programs for their pursuit constitute unit plans that are reviewed at one or more higher levels. In these reviews plans prepared at different levels are integrated, and those prepared at the same level are coordinated.

The effectiveness of preactive planning clearly depends on the accuracy of the forecasts for which it prepares. Unfortunately, such forecasts are chronically in error. The reason is that the only things we can predict accurately (in principle as well as practice) are aspects of the future that will not be affected by what we and others do (for example, the weather). But preactive planning is based on forecasts of supplier, consumer, and competitive behavior as well as economic, social, and political conditions, all of which are affected by what is done by organizations that plan and those that do not. This logically requires an endless repetition of the prediction–preparation cycle. Since this is not possible, whatever predictions are used do not take into account the effects of the plans based on them. For this reason, among others, significant portions of the forecast are bound to be in error.

Moreover, even those aspects of an organization's future that are not affected by what it and others do (e.g., the weather) cannot be forecasted well for more than a short period. As in the case of the weather, however, the need to forecast it can be eliminated by bringing it under *control*, as we do by building structures within which work can proceed whatever the external weather may be.

Interactive Planning

Interactive planning is directed at gaining control of the future. It is based on the belief that an organization's future depends at least as much on what it does between now and then as on what is done to it. Therefore, this type of planning consists of *the design of a desirable future and the selection or invention of ways of bringing it about as closely as possible.*

Reactive, Preactive, and Interactive Planners

Reactive planners focus on increasing their ability to undo changes that have already occurred. Preactive planners focus on increasing their ability to forecast changes that will occur. Interactive planners focus on increasing their ability to control or influence change or its effects, and to respond rapidly and effectively to changes they cannot control, thereby decreasing their need to forecast.

Reactive planning is primarily concerned with removal of threats; preactive planning is concerned with exploitation of opportunities. Interactive planning is concerned with both equally but it assumes that threats and opportunities are created by what an organization does as well as by what is done to it.

Reactive planners try to do well enough, to "satisfice," to enable the organization planned for to *survive*. Preactive planners try to do as well as possible, to "optimize," to enable the organization planned for to *grow*. Interactive planners try to do better in the future than the best that is currently possible, to "idealize," to enable the organization planned for to *develop*. An organization develops when it increases its ability and desire to satisfy the needs and desires of those who depend on it, its stakeholders.

We now consider the characteristics of interactive planning in more detail by focusing on what might be called its "operating principles."

OPERATING PRINCIPLES OF INTERACTIVE PLANNING

There are three such principles: *the participative principle, the principle of continuity, and the holistic principle.*

The Participative Principle

The most important (but not the only) benefit of planning is not derived from use of its product, a plan, but from engaging in its production. In interactive planning, process is the most important product. By engaging in this process its participants come to understand their organization and its environment, and how their behavior can improve performance of the whole, not just their part of it. It is this increase in the ability of each part of an organization to contribute to improvement of overall performance that is the principal benefit of planning.

Effective planning cannot be done *to* or *for* an organization; it must be done *by* it. Therefore, the proper role of the professional planner, whether inside or outside an organization, is *not* to plan for others, but to encourage and facilitate their planning for themselves. All those who are part of an organization and all those external to it who are affected by it (except competitors) should be given an opportunity to participate in its planning. The professional planner should provide all these stakeholders with the information, knowledge, understanding, and motivation that can enable them to plan more effectively than they would otherwise.

The Principle of Continuity

All plans are based on a large number of assumptions. An assumption is a proposition that we treat as though it were true; we act on it. It differs from a forecast; for example, we carry a spare tire in our cars because we assume we may have a flat tire but we do not predict that we will have one. Nevertheless, an assumption may be based on a forecast, as when we assume it will rain tomorrow because that is the forecast. On the other hand, we can (and often do) assume that a forecast is wrong.

Because organizations and their environments change continually over time, planners should explicitly formulate as many as possible of their relevant assumptions about what will, will not, can, and cannot change. They should monitor these assumptions continually. When they are found to be in error, plans should be modified appropriately, that is, adapted to changing assumptions. Such adaptation must be continuous if the effectiveness of plans is to be maintained or, more important, increased.

To maximize the learning and adaptation of planners, planning decisions should be implemented experimentally, that is, in as controlled a way as possible. This facilitates frequent comparisons of a plan's actual performance with explicitly formulated expectations. Where actual and expected performance differ significantly, the causes of the deviations should be identified and appropriate corrective action taken.

The Holistic Principle

This principle has two parts: the *principle of coordination* and the *principle of integration*. Each has to do with a different dimension of organization. Organizations are divided into levels, and each level (except possibly the top) is divided into units that are differentiated by function, type of output, market, or some combination of these. Coordination has to do with the interactions of units at the same level, integration with interactions of units at different levels.

The Principle of Coordination

The principle of coordination asserts that all parts of an organization at the same level should be planned for simultaneously and interdependently. This follows from the fact that the sources of threats and opportunities frequently are not located where their symptoms appear. Therefore, no part or aspect of a particular level of an organization can be planned for effectively if planned for independently of any other part or aspect of that level. For example, reduction of the cost of production may require redesign of products or changes in the mix of sales; a change in the sales mix may require a change in the way salesmen are compensated. In planning, breadth is more important than depth, and interactions are more important than actions.

The Principle of Integration

The principle of integration asserts that planning done independently at any level of an organization cannot be effective; all levels should be planned for simultaneously and interdependently. It is commonplace for a practice or policy established at one level of an organization to create problems at another level. Therefore, the solution of a problem that appears at one level may best be obtained by changing a policy or a practice established at another level.

When the principles of coordination and integration are combined the *holistic principle* is obtained: every part of an organization at every level should plan simultaneously and interdependently. The concept of all-over-at-once planning differs significantly from both reactive bottom-up and preactive top-down planning.

THE FIVE PHASES OF INTERACTIVE PLANNING

1. **Formulation of the mess.** Determination of what problems and opportunities face the organization planned for, how they interact, and what obstructs or constrains the organization's doing something about

them. The output of this phase takes the form of a *reference scenario*.

2. **Ends planning.**   Determination of what is wanted by means of an *idealized redesign* of the system planned for. Goals, objectives, and ideals are extracted from this design. Comparison of the reference scenario and the idealized redesign identifies the gaps to be closed or narrowed by the planning process.

3. **Means planning.**   Determination of what should be done to close or narrow the gaps. This requires selecting or inventing appropriate courses of action, practices, projects, programs, and policies.

4. **Resource planning.**   Determination of what types of resource and how much of each will be required by the means chosen, when they will be required, and how they are to be acquired or generated.

5. **Implementation and Control.**   Determination of who is to do what, when it is to be done, and how to assure that these assignments and schedules are carried out as expected and produce the desired effects on performance.

These five phases of interactive planning, as seen in Figure 1.1, usually interact; they all can take place simultaneously. The order in which they are presented is the one in which they are usually, but not invariably, initiated. In continuous planning, none of them is ever completed.

Before discussing each of these phases in turn, we will consider how the planning process should be organized.

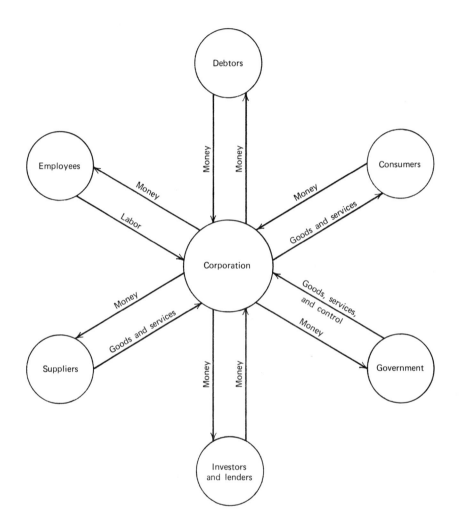

Figure 1.1
An interactive planning cycle.

CHAPTER TWO

Organization of the Planning Effort

■   ■   ■

PLANNING TEAMS

Each unit of the organization should form a planning team consisting of all the members of the unit who want to participate
in it.

> We believe participation should be voluntary because under this
> condition the extent of participation reveals how effective and im-
> portant the members of the unit consider it to be. For the same rea-
> son, members of the planning teams should be free to discontinue
> their participation at any time, and members of the unit who have
> not participated should be free to join the team whenever they
> want to. Ideally, of course, every member of the unit would partici-
> pate voluntarily.

Each planning team can, without external approval, make
any decision that affects only its unit and for which it has the
resources required.

Any decision that a team makes that affects any other unit at
the same or a higher level must be approved by the lowest-level
planning board (described below) to which all the affected units
report. The plan prepared at any level but the top should be reviewed by the planning board at the next higher level to determine whether there are any such effects.

Any decision that affects lower-level units should be reviewed by these units and their reactions should be taken into account before plans are settled. The board of the unit that prepares a plan should determine whether lower-level units are
affected and their reactions adequately considered.

Any planning team can make recommendations to any other
unit. The board of the unit receiving the recommendations

should determine whether they have received adequate consideration.

PLANNING BOARDS

Every unit other than those that have no subordinate units should have a planning board. (See Figure 2.1) Such Boards should consist of:

1. The manager of that unit.
2. The manager's immediate subordinates (the managers who report directly to him or her).
3. The manager's immediate superior (the manager to whom he or she reports directly).

In a matrix organization there may be more than one immediate superior. At the top of the organization there is no superior. The top planning board should include representatives of the corporate board and as many external stakeholders as possible.

If a unit contains more than about ten people it should be be subdivided into planning teams of approximately equal size. Each should prepare a plan for the whole unit. Synthesis of the plans they produce should be carried out by the unit's planning board. If the unit so affected is at the lowest level, it too should have a planning board consisting of the head of each planning team, the unit manager, and his immediate superior.

Every planning board other than those set up for units at the top and bottom levels will have three levels of management represented on it, and all managers other than those at the top and bottom will serve on boards at three levels: their immediate superior's, their own, and their immediate subordinates'. Those

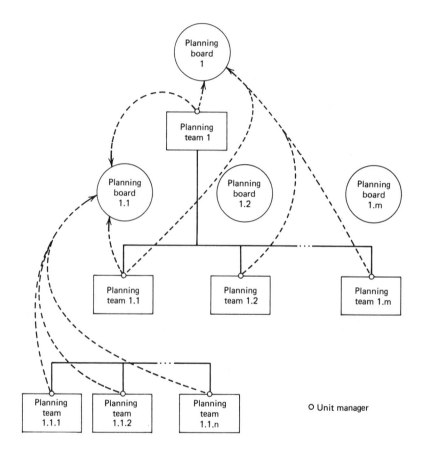

Figure 2.1
Organization of the planning process.

managers at other than the top or bottom will interact with as many as five levels of management on these boards: two higher levels and their own on their superior's board, and two lower levels on their subordinates' boards. These multilevel boards make possible effective integration and coordination of plans prepared by different units at the same and different levels of the organization.

Planning boards should organize themselves as they see fit, for example, with permanent or rotating chairpersons. Planning teams should be organized by the managers of the units planned for. Both boards and teams should meet frequently enough to sustain continuous planning.

Any part of an organization can install such a planning system as is described here even if the rest of the organization does not.

Although simultaneous and interdependent planning in every part of an organization is desirable, it is possible to plan sequentially, either from the top down or the bottom up. In either of these cases it is important that no plans be made final until reactions to it are obtained from units that subsequently engage in planning.

The design presented here is easily adapted to other than conventionally organized corporations, for example, to matrix and multidimensional structures.

The kind of participation in planning that this design makes possible goes a long way toward improving the quality of working life at all levels of an organization. Moreover, as stated in the earlier discussion of the participative principle, it enables each member of the organization to gain understanding of how his activities affect the performance of the organization as a whole. This makes it possible for every part of the whole to contribute more effectively to the performance of the whole. Increase of this ability is the principal benefit to be derived from interactive planning.

CHAPTER THREE

Formulating
the Mess

■ ▪ ■

A mess is a system of interrelated threats and opportunities. Formulation of a mess consists of identifying those current and future threats and opportunities, and their interactions, that derive from the recent and current behavior of the organization planned for and its environment.

Three types of study are needed as inputs to the formulation of a mess:

1. **Systems analysis.** What the organization is, how it operates, and its current state.
2. **Obstruction analysis.** What internal and external conditions, policies, and practices obstruct organizational development.
3. **Reference projections.** What will happen if there are no significant changes in the behavior of the organization and its environment.

These studies can be carried out relatively independently, but once completed, they should be synthesized into a *reference scenario*. This is a comprehensive description of the likely future of the organization should there be no significant changes in its own behavior and that of its environment.

SYSTEMS ANALYSIS

A systems analysis is a description of the current nature and state of the organization planned for. It should cover the following aspects of the organization and its environment:

1. The nature of the business.
2. Its past and present performance.
3. The business environment.
4. The structure of the organization.
5. Its management style.
6. Its rules of the game.
7. Its personnel policies and practices.
8. Its operations.

Initial study of these areas need not be deep or detailed; breadth is more important than depth at this stage. Subsequent steps in the planning process may require more intensive study of at least some of these areas.

Now consider each of these aspects of the organization in a little more detail.

The Nature of the Business

The business that the organization is in should be identified. If the entity planned for is part of a larger organization, the business of that organization and the function of the part should be described. Definition of the business should be general enough to include all the products and services it offers. This will require reference to one or more of the following characteristics:

1. Structural characteristics of its products (e.g., petroleum or aluminum products, or electric motors).
2. Process characteristics (e.g., refining or baking).
3. Functional characteristics of its products or services (e.g., metalworking equipment or pet food).
4. The markets it serves (e.g., retail food stores or gasoline stations).

Past and Present Performance

An analysis should be made of the organization's total sales, overall profitability, sales volume, market share, earnings, return on investment and assets, costs by category, and so on. Similar analyses should then be carried out for product and market categories. The results of such analyses are usually best shown on graphs.

The Business Environment

Current and potential regulations, laws, and taxes that affect the organization, and their effects on it, should be identified; for example, container legislation, accelerated depreciation allowances, and increased excise taxes. Special interest groups, such as consumerists and environmentalists, that are having or can have an effect on the organization, and the nature of these effects should also be identified. Conversely, the effects of the organization's behavior on its social and physical environment should also be described.

The main competitors of the organization should be identified by product or service categories and by markets where relevant. Information should be obtained on the size of competitors, their shares of markets, changes in these shares over time, and their pricing, quality, and innovation policies.

A stakeholder is any noncompetitive individual or organization directly affected by the organization's behavior and performance; for example, stockholders, suppliers, customers, government, communities in which facilities are located, creditors, unions, distributors, and retailers. Stakeholders should be identified and characterized by properties that affect the organization's performance; for example, the number of customers, per capita consumption of the organization's products or services, and when, where, and how these are used.

Special attention should be given to the organization's suppliers of those raw materials and/or services on which it is most dependent. This analysis should include such information as the number, size, and location of suppliers, their reliability, and how dependent they are on the organization's business.

The Organization's Structure

A detailed chart of the current organizational structure should be prepared. The responsibilities of each unit should be described in detail. Any overlap of responsibilities should be noted. Most important, differences between the way organization is supposed to work and the way it does should be noted; that is, the informal organization should also be described.

Management Style

Such questions as the following should be answered: How are problems identified, decisions made, implemented, and controlled? What types of decision are centralized and what types are decentralized? Do those with responsibility have the authority they need? Who is accountable for what? Is management autocratic or participative, formal or informal, and what perquisites does it have? How effectively is information communicated up, down, and across the organization?

Rules of the Game

The implicit and explicit policies and practices that prevail in or are imposed on the organization should be spelled out. This should be done for the organization as a whole, and separately for each of its dispersed units. The following are examples of one company's rules of the game:

1. All appointments to managerial positions above a specified level should be from within.
2. Unions should be avoided.
3. Wages and salaries should be 20 percent higher than those offered by competition.
4. Be a price leader.
5. Follow rather than lead with innovations.

Personnel Policies and Practices

The policies and practices applied to recruiting, hiring, orientation of new employees, assignment, reassignment, compensation, training and education, promotion, firing, quitting, and retirement as they apply to each level should be described. In addition, all benefits and incentives should be identified. If at all possible, attitudes of personnel in every category at all levels toward the organization, their work, and the work environment should be determined.

Operations

A set of flow charts and supporting descriptive material should be prepared to cover the following aspects of the organization's operations.

1. Flow charts should be prepared to show the sources and flow of information, instruction, and material.

   a. The initial charts should show each step in the process. (See Figures 3.1. and 3.2.) At this stage too much detail is not possible.

b. At each location at which something is done, inputs of information, instruction, material, or product and the capacity and current level of operations should be noted.

c. The initial charts should subsequently be consolidated by putting together all operations that are subject to the same controls. If a single instruction covers a sequence of steps shown in the original charts, these should be combined and given an appropriate name even if separate organizational units are involved. (See Figure 3.3.) For example, if all production lots are processed over the same sequence of machines, that sequence can be shown as a single production operation with a capacity equal to that of the step in the sequence with the lowest capacity.

2. Flow charts or descriptions should be prepared for each organizational unit (other than finance) that has not appeared in the output of step 1; for example, personnel, legal, and environmental affairs.

3. A flow chart should be prepared showing the flow of money from its various sources into and through the organization planned for, and from there to its various destinations. It should also show where financial decisions are made and transmitted, and how the information used in making these decisions is supplied.

OBSTRUCTION ANALYSIS

The purpose of an obstruction analysis is to identify internally

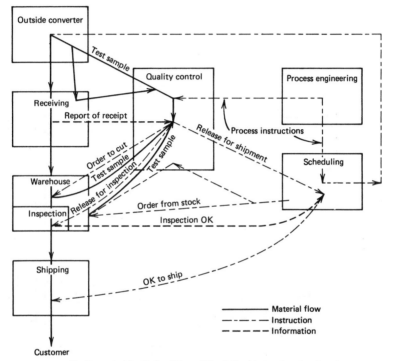

Figure 3.1
An example of initial notes in a systems analysis.

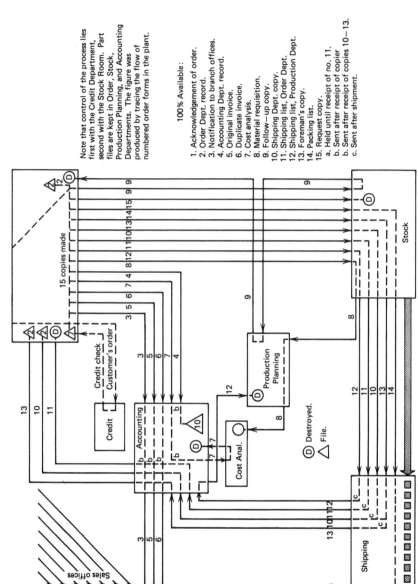

Figure 3.2

An example of a detailed systems analysis of a parts ordering process in a machine tool manufacturing company.

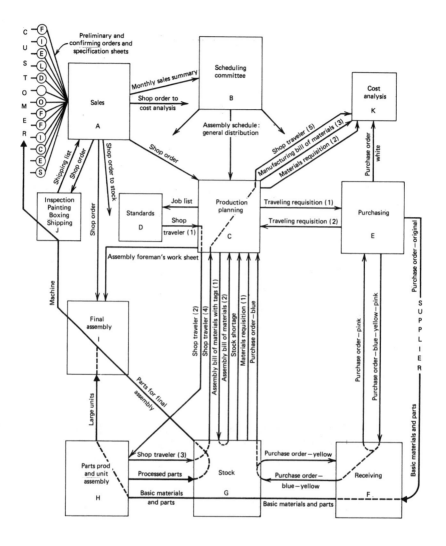

Figure 3.3

An example of a consolidated flow chart of machine
tool production.

and externally imposed constraints that obstruct the development of the organization planned for.

Internal Obstructions

There are two types of such obstructions: discrepancies between what an organization practices and what it preaches, and internal conflicts.

Internal discrepancies can be identified by use of brainstorming sessions in which a list of norms and beliefs that prevail in the organization is formulated and discussed. These norms and beliefs may relate to any of the subjects listed in the section on systems analysis and, in addition, ends (goals, objectives, and ideals), means employed to pursue these ends, and resources available for such pursuits. Examples of such discrepancies are given in Table 3.1.

Internal conflicts are of several types each of which should be looked for during obstruction analysis.

1. **Conflicts between individuals.** Conflicts arise in any group whose members interact a great deal. Some such conflicts are due to differences in personality, others to disagreements over ends, means, and allocation of resources.

2. **Conflicts between individuals and the organization or parts of it.** These manifest themselves in employee dissatisfaction, alienation, and poor morale. At lower levels, such conflicts are frequently reflected in absenteeism, lateness, accidents, sabotage, unionization efforts, strikes, or filing of grievances.

3. **Conflicts within units.** These usually derive from the assignment of conflicting objectives to the unit from higher-level authorities. For example, a production unit

Table 3.1.

Examples of Discrepancies

	Preached	Practiced
Ends	Be a good corporate citizen.	Do as little for the community as you can get away with.
	Equal opportunity employment.	Make no effort to recruit minorities but give those that apply equal treatment.
Means	Diversity through product innovation.	Diversify through acquisition or imitation.
	Care about employees.	Minimize employment.
Management	Long-range stategic planning.	Crisis management.
Resources	Get the best people available.	Maintain salaries at the industry's average.
	Keep plants up-to-date and in top condition.	Maintain and replace equipment only when absolutely necessary.
Environment	A commitment to quality.	Sacrifice quality when necessary to make price attractive.
	Concern and respect for consumers.	Advertise to them as though they were simple-minded.

may be told to minimize both its finished-goods inven-
tories and the number of orders it cannot fill from stock.
Unless units assigned conflicting objectives are provided
with explicit criteria for finding an acceptable balance
between them, performance will suffer.

4. Conflicts between units at the same level.
Objectives are frequently assigned to units at the same
level that put them into conflict with each other. For
example, a production department may be instructed to

minimize production costs and a sales department to maximize sales. The product mix that does one of these seldom does the other.

5. **Conflicts between units at different levels.** These conflicts often involve allocation of resources, or practices and policies issued from above. The imposition of reporting, accounting, and administrative procedures that effectively serve one level of an organization often obstruct units at lower levels.

6. **Conflicts within the organization as a whole.** Corporations, for example, frequently have conflicting objectives such as "good employee relations" and "minimization of the work force."

External Obstructions

Potential as well as actual conflicts with external stakeholders —governments, communities, stockholders, suppliers, unions, customers, and special interest groups—should be identified. The organization's current and currently planned activities directed at affecting these conflicts should be described.

REFERENCE PROJECTIONS

A reference projection is an extrapolation of a performance characteristic of an organization, its parts, or its environment from its recent past into the future, assuming no significant changes in the behavior of the system or its environment. These are *not* forecasts of the future; they are "what if" projections. They reveal those current objectives that cannot possibly be attained without a change in either the organization's behavior or that of its environment. For example, if saturation of a company's market is approaching, it cannot continue to grow unless it either enlarges its market or expands its product line.

Reference projections can also reveal future needs that will not be able to be satisfied unless there is a change in what the organization or its competitors are currently doing. For example, such projections made in 1959 and 1970 clearly showed that sales of automobiles could not continue at their then current rates unless automobile size was reduced (Sagasti and Ackoff, 1971).

There is no mechanical way of determining what corporate and environmental characteristics should be used in preparing reference projections. It is usually fruitful to begin with the most important measures of organizational performance and critical assumptions about the environment.

Measures of Performance

The trends of different measures of performance and the relationships between them often reveal potential problems or crises. Comparisons between the level of sales and the values of different types of assets (e.g., fixed, inventory, accounts receivable, and total) are sometimes revealing. Rapid increases in the ratio of assets to sales forebodes danger. Comparison with the average ratio in the relevant industry, or with those of major competitors, can also indicate potential trouble.

Plots of various measures of profitability over time and their extrapolations can also be useful; for example, profit margin (net profit after taxes/sales), return on investment (net profit after taxes/total assets), and return on net worth (net profit after taxes/net worth). There are, of course, other measures of profitability that can be used. By studying trends of these measures and comparing them with those of major competitors and that of the relevant industry as a whole, one can see whether trends of costs and prices are in line.

Products have a life cycle: introduction, rapid growth, slower growth, maturity, decline, and replacement (Figure 3.4). New technology or design is often responsible for terminating growth or maturity. Analysis of sales trends and comparison with those of major competitors and the relevant industry as a whole can reveal potential threats and crises. These studies can also be conducted for specific models, package sizes, and market areas. They can indicate future trouble spots that would be missed in a macroscopic analysis.

The relationships of earnings or costs to time and the ratio of either to sales can indicate if and when things are going out of control. Earnings and costs seldom increase linearly with increases in sales. An increase of earnings that is less rapid than that of sales, or an increase of costs more rapid than sales, indicates a potential problem. The relationship between such measures as assets and earnings and earnings and sales can also be revealing.

Where possible, at least ten years of past data should be plotted. These plots should then be extrapolated over approximately the same number of years. Such extrapolations can be made using standard statistical procedures, but "the naked eye and bare hand" are often good enough.

Assumptions

It is usually worth exploring the critical assumptions about the organization and its environment on which the organization's expectations of the future are based. Such assumptions seldom are explicitly formulated, hence analysis of the organization's expectations is required to get at them. Once exposed, these assumptions can be used to prepare a set of projections to reveal their consequences. In some cases, the consequences implied

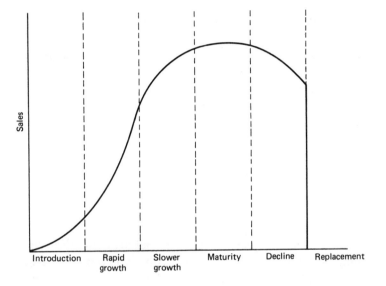

Figure 3.4
Product life cycle.

by assumptions are not possible and, therefore, reveal the un-
tenability of the assumptions. For example, to accommodate
the number of automobiles that would be in use in the year 2000,
assuming continuation of the growth experienced in the 1960s
and no change in the size of the automobile, would require
covering more than the total surface of all U.S. cities. This
showed that maintenance, let alone growth, of automobile sales
was not possible unless the size of cars was reduced.

Availability of critical inputs (e.g., materials, facilities, personnel, etc.) and the use of the organization's outputs should
also be explored. For example, the office space required to clear
checks at a branch of the Federal Reserve Bank, assuming continuation of the then current rate of increase in use of checks,
was found to exceed the space available in that bank's head-
quarter city. This revelation led the bank to explore, and eventually to introduce, the Electronic Funds Transfer system.

REFERENCE SCENARIO

Those reference projections that turn out to be revealing can be
combined with the outputs of the system and obstruction analyses to form a scenario of the future that the organization would
be likely to have if its behavior and that of its environment were
not to change in any significant way. It is in such a scenario
that the organizational mess is best revealed.

A reference scenario can reveal the crises inherent in current
policies and practices. Put another way: it is a description of
the crises that the organization would face if it failed to learn
from its own experience and adapt to environmental changes.

The following procedure can be used in preparing such a
scenario.

1. Set a time horizon as many years out into the future as were used back into the past in extrapolating the future.

2. Prepare a summary of the main performance indicators (past and extrapolated). This information can be extracted from the reference projections.

3. Summarize relevant current trends in supply of required resources, competitive behavior, consumption, and government behavior.

4. Prepare a table in which the trends form the rows and the performance indicators form the columns. Indicate in each relevant box whether the trend will have a positive or negative effect on the performance measure, and whether this is likely to be strong, moderate, or weak. If there is no effect, leave the box blank.

5. Place yourself at the time horizon and write a prose description of the organization and its environment at the time and how it got there. Preparation of this description requires use of the information obtained from the systems and obstruction analyses as well as the reference projections.

In effect, the reference scenario is a prospective history of the organization's future out to the horizon. Remember that this is not a forecast of that future. The fact that a reference scenario is being prepared in the context of interactive planning is a denial of one of the assumptions on which the scenario is based: no changes in the organization's policies and practices.

Examples of reference scenarios are provided in Chapter 8.

CHAPTER FOUR

Ends Planning

Ends planning consists of designing a desired future and extracting from it those ends that the rest of the planning process is addressed to pursuing.

Ends are desired outcomes and are of three types:

1. **Goals.** Ends that are expected to be obtained within the period covered by the plan.
2. **Objectives.** Ends that are not expected to be obtained until after the period planned for, but towards which progress is expected during this period.
3. **Ideals.** Ends that are believed to be unattainable, but towards which continuous progress is thought to be possible and is expected.

Therefore, goals can be considered to be means with respect to objectives, and objectives can be similarly considered with respect to ideals.

Ends planning involves four steps:

1. Selecting a mission.
2. Specifying desired properties of the system planned for.
3. Idealized redesign of that system.
4. Selecting the gaps between this design and the reference scenario which planning will try to close.

Each of these steps is now considered in turn.

SELECTING A MISSION

A mission is an overriding purpose that can unify and mobilize all parts of the organization planned for. The formulation of the

41 ∎

mission should be challenging and exciting to virtually all of an organization's stakeholders. It should also provide a focus for the planning process that follows.

A mission statement should identify the business in which the organization *wants to be*. This may differ from the business it is in. The statement should also specify what effects it wants to have on each class of its stakeholders.

Examples of mission statements are provided in Chapter 9.

SPECIFYING DESIRED PROPERTIES OF THE SYSTEM PLANNED FOR

The desired properties of a system can usually be identified in brainstorming sessions. Such sessions should not be constrained by considerations of feasibility. The properties specified should be those that the participants believe the organization planned for should *ideally* have *now*. A distinction should be made between those properties on which a consensus is reached and those on which there is a significant difference of opinion.

The following are a few of the specifications once prepared for an idealized telephone system.

1. There would be no wrong numbers.
2. You would know who is calling before answering the phone.
3. The phone could be used without hands.
4. You would not have to go to the phone; it would come to you.
5. You could arrange to receive calls placed to your home or office even when you are not there.

6. When you are on the phone and someone is trying to reach you, you would know who it is and would be able to deliver a message to them without interrupting the current call.

Specification of desired properties can be facilitated by using the following checklist of aspects of the organization or unit planned for. The list may have to be modified to fit some organizations.

1. **Inputs.** Five types of resource should be considered: plants and equipment, materials and energy, people, information, and money. For each of these the following questions should be asked.

   a. What is required?

   b. Should it be acquired from an external or internal source?

   c. For those resources to be acquired, from what sources should they be acquired and how? (The possibility of vertical integration should be considered.)

2. **The corporate process.**

   a. Who should own the organization and what should their role be?

   b. Which functions necessary for organizational activity should be provided by the organization itself and which should be acquired from external sources?

   c. How should the organization be structured and managed?

   d. In particular, what policies and practices should apply to personnel with respect to recruiting, hiring, orientation, compensation and incentives, benefits, promotions, career development, retirement, and severance?

    e. What should be the nature of the production processes and how should they be designed and organized?

3. **Products and services.**

    a. What products or services should the corporation offer and what special characteristics, if any, should they have?

    b. How should internal development of products or services be organized and carried out?

    c. How should acquisition be organized and carried out?

4. **Markets and customers.**

    a. What types of customer should the corporation seek?

    b. In which market areas?

    c. How should its products or services be distributed and sold?

    d. How should its products or services be marketed and, in the case of products, be serviced?

5. **The environment.**

    a. How should the organization relate to its stakeholders (including government and unions) and the communities in which it operates?

    b. How should information on stakeholders' perceptions of the organization be obtained and used?

    c. How should the organization relate to environmental, consumer, and other special interest groups?

Examples of property specifications are provided in Chapter 10.

IDEALIZED REDESIGN OF THE SYSTEM

An ideally redesigned system is one with which the designers would *now* replace the existing system if they were free to re-place it with any system they wanted. Such redesign is subject to only two constraints.

1. The design must be *technologically feasible*; that is, it cannot incorporate any technology that is not known to be feasible at the time the design is produced.

2. The design must be *operationally viable*; that is, it must be capable of operating in the current environment of the system planned for. However, no consideration should be given to the feasibility of implementing the ideally redesigned system because doing this constrains creativity. Moreover, the total design may be feasible even though it contains parts that are infeasible when considered separately.

Three principles should be followed in the idealized design process.

1. Where there is no objective basis for making a design decision, the system should be designed so that it can determine experimentally which of the available alternatives is the best. (This applies to properties on which consensus is not reached.) For example, if the designers have no basis for deciding which of two possible new practices to include in their design, they should incorporate an experimental comparison of both.

2. The system should be designed so it can continuously evaluate features that have been designed into it and decisions that are made within it. This enables it to *learn* efficiently.

3. Since any design incorporates assumptions about the future, the system should be designed to monitor these assumptions and to modify itself appropriately when an

assumption turns out to be false. This enables it to *adapt* effectively.

The first two of these principles assure the design of a system that is capable of effective learning. The third assures its ability to adapt well to changing conditions. Therefore, the product of an idealized design is an *adaptive-learning system*. The output is neither utopian nor ideal because it is subject to improvement. It is the best *ideal-seeking system* that its designers can conceptualize *now*, but not necessarily later.

The idealized design process is initiated by producing "bits of design" around the properties identified in the second step of ends planning. Several procedures can be used to stimulate the generation of innovative ideas: brainstorming, synectics, dialectics, and so on. (See Ackoff and Vergara, 1981.)

Once the design elements have been completed, they should be checked for their technological, but no other kind of, feasibility. Where such feasibility is not apparent, experts should be consulted.

Now the various design elements can be assembled into a scenario, a comprehensive and coordinated picture of the desired whole. Examples of such a scenario are provided in Chapter 11.

Note that whether or not the organization or unit being designed is autonomous, its design is constrained by the nature of the system that contains it. Therefore, it is desirable to prepare two separate but interrelated designs: one that accepts the constraints imposed by the containing system and one that does not. In preparing the unconstrained design any aspect of the containing system that affects the design of the contained system can be changed. Discussion of these two designs with managers of the containing system often can induce some of the changes desired. It is preferable to prepare the constrained design first, then to improve it by eliminating any undesirable constraints.

COMPARING THE REFERENCE SCENARIO AND THE IDEALIZED DESIGN

Once a consensus version of the constrained idealized design is obtained it can be compared with the reference scenario. This comparison will yield a set of differences that constitute the gaps between what would happen if things were to continue as they are and what the organization would most like. These gaps should be listed using the classification scheme given in the section on specifying desired properties of the system planned for.

Selecting the Gaps to Be Filled

The gaps listed should be classified as goals, objectives, and ideals. This classification may later have to be revised because of information subsequently obtained. Once this classification has been completed, means planning can be initiated.

CHAPTER FIVE

Means Planning

A *means* is behavior that either produces a desired outcome or brings one closer to it. Like ends, means are of different types:

1. **Acts.** Things that take relatively little time to do—for example, standing up, making a phone call, or mailing a letter.

2. **Course of action, process, or procedure.** A sequence of acts directed at producing a desired outcome—for example, taking a trip, negotiating a contract, installing a new piece of equipment, or manufacturing an automobile.

3. **Practice.** A frequently repeated act or course of action—for example, filling out travel vouchers, preparing monthly reports, or punching a time clock.

4. **Project.** A system of simultaneous and/or sequential courses of action directed at one or more desired outcomes—for example, erecting a building, moving from one place to another, or developing a new product.

5. **Program.** A system of projects directed at one or more desired outcomes—for example, developing a new product line, expanding into new markets, or vertically integrating.

There is nothing absolute about these categories but they usually differ with respect to their duration and the generality of the ends at which they are directed.

A choice of means is a *decision*, and a rule for making a specified class of decisions is a *policy*, for example, promoting only from within.

Means planning is concerned with finding or inventing ways of approximating the idealized design as closely as possible. It involves formulating or identifying potential means, and evaluating the alternatives and selecting the best. The choice can be recorded on a form such as is shown in Figure 5.1. It includes:

1. Goals or objectives addressed.
2. A description of the means selected.
3. Expected effects of the means and when they are expected.
4. Critical assumptions on which these expectations are based.
5. Critical information used in selecting the means and its sources.
6. A brief description of how the means was selected and by whom.

All of this is useful for control purposes. Without such a record, control and learning from one's choices is very difficult.

FORMULATION OR IDENTIFICATION OF ALTERNATIVE MEANS

A means consists of changing the values of one or more controllable variables. The effects of such changes (i.e., the outcomes produced) depend on uncontrolled (environmental) variables. Changes of the values of controlled and uncontrolled variables are frequently limited or constrained as, for example, when there are price controls or when rationing is in effect.

A choice of means involves:

1. **People.** The *person* or *group* that desires either to bring about a change that is not otherwise expected to

Date:

1. Goals or objectives addressed:

2. Brief description of means selected:

3. Expected effects and when they are expected:

4. Critical assumptions on which this choice was made:

5. Critical information used in selecting this means and its sources:

6. Brief description of how the means was selected and by whom:

Figure 5.1
Record of means selected.

occur, or to prevent a change that is otherwise expected to occur.

2. **Ends.**   Desired outcomes of the choice.

3. **Means.**   Behavior defined by changes of the values of controlled variables.

4. **The environment.**   The set of uncontrolled variables that, together with the controlled variables, produce the outcome of the choice.

5. **Constraints.**   Limits on the values of controlled and uncontrolled variables.

The formulation or identification of means requires answering the following questions:

1. What variables are relevant and subject to control, and what constraints apply to them?

2. What variables are relevant but not subject to control, and what constraints apply to them?

3. How do the controlled and uncontrolled variables interact to produce an outcome?

Dramatic improvements in organizational performance are seldom obtained by using an obvious means; they follow from finding or inventing ones superior to any that are apparent. Creative and effective formulation of means consists of identifying and removing *self-imposed* constraints that prevent finding good answers to the three questions listed above. (For ways of identifying and removing such constraints, see Ackoff, 1978.)

Selecting Relevant Controllable Variables

The following are some suggestions as to how to arrive at this selection more creatively and effectively.

1. Involve people with as many different types of background and experience as possible. Different points of view help to reveal different types of controllable variables. Economists, for example, tend to see only economic variables; production managers, only production variables; financial managers, only financial variables; and so on.

2. Use creativity-enhancing techniques in the groups brought together to formulate and identify means; for example, synectics, TKJ, search conferences, lateral thinking, brainstorming, and dialectics. (See Ackoff and Vergara, 1981.)

3. Look at the choice to be made in the largest possible context, not the smallest. Cutting choice situations down to size frequently precludes consideration of effective means. Therefore, look for means in the largest system on which you have some influence. If you do not succeed, descend to the next smaller system, and so on.

Controlling Uncontrolled Variables

Variables that appear to be uncontrollable can frequently be brought under control, at least partially, in one or more of the following ways:

1. Vertical integration. Incorporation of an uncontrolled variable into the system planned for so as to bring it under control; for example, an automobile company initiating steel production to assure its supply of this material at a controllable cost.

2. Horizontal integration. Enlargement of a system to enable it to control the effects of an uncontrolled variable without controlling that variable itself; for example, hedging purchases on a commodity exchange to

eliminate the effect of price changes in the time between purchase and delivery.

3. **Coalitions.** Cooperation with others to control or influence something that no one of the cooperators acting separately can influence or control, as when an industrial association lobbies for or against proposed legislation or establishes standards for its industry.

4. **Incentives.** Use of incentives or disincentives to induce desirable behavior or inhibit undesirable behavior in some organizations or individuals who are not subject to control; for example, inducing sales by price-promotions, or productivity by offering bonuses to employees.

5. **Responsiveness.** Minimizing the effects of uncontrolled variables by increasing the ability of the system to respond rapidly and effectively to whatever occurs as, for example, preparing contingency plans or equipping oneself to handle emergencies.

Relating Variables to Outcomes

The selection of variables to be controlled and the identification of relevant uncontrolled variables are based on which variables one believes to be *causally* related to desired outcomes and what one assumes about their interactions.

Causal relationships are too frequently assumed to exist where they do not; variables that are known to be *associated* are incorrectly assumed to be causally related. Correlation and regression coefficients (and their derivatives) are the principal measures of association. Even where these are found to be statistically significant, causal connections cannot legitimately be inferred from them.

The only causal inference that can be justified by use of correlation or regression analysis is: two variables are *not* causally related if (1) they are *not* significantly associated, (2) the conditions under which they are not associated persist, and (3) the form of the association (e.g., linear, quadratic, or exponential) assumed in determining that they are not associated is correct or approximately so.

Establishment of a causal connection between two variables requires demonstration that in some specified environment either (1) a change in one (the product) cannot occur unless there is a preceding or simultaneous change in the other (the producer), or (2) a change in one (the cause) is invariably followed by a change in the other (the effect). That is, one change causes another only if the first can be shown to be either *necessary* or *sufficient* for the other. This is often difficult to establish but, difficult or not, is essential for correctly inferring a causal connection. This can best be done by experimentation.

Experimentation is often incorrectly assumed to be too costly or impractical, if not infeasible. The cost of *not* conducting experiments often exceeds that of conducting them, and their apparent infeasibility is often due to lack of knowledge of the variety of experimental designs that are available. (See, for example, Mendenhall, 1968, and Campbell and Stanley, 1966.)

EVALUATION OF ALTERNATIVE MEANS

The evaluation of means should be carried out so as to take as little time as possible, cost as little as possible, produce accurate and reliable evaluations, and maximize what is learned from the process.

Whenever possible, means should be evaluated before they are used. The decision whether or not to do so should be based on balancing two costs:

1. The cost of the delay required to carry out the evaluation, assuming the means are as good as expected, plus the cost of the evaluation itself.

2. The expected cost of implementing the means if it per-
   forms less well than expected.

These costs depend on how reversible the decision to implement is, and the duration and magnitude of its effects.

If a means is not evaluated prior to its implementation, then
a procedure should be designed for monitoring its effects after
its implementation. Such monitoring should include the following steps:

1. An explicit formulation of the outcomes expected from
   use of the means and specification of when they are
   expected.
2. An explicit formulation of the assumptions on which the
   expected effects are based.
3. Collection of information on the assumed conditions and
   actual performance.
4. Comparison of actual and predicted performance and
   actual and assumed conditions, and identification of
   significant deviations.
5. When significant deviations are found, design and implementation of appropriate corrective action.

The Use of Models in Evaluating Means

As previously indicated, the most effective way of evaluating a
means is by experimentation, but this is not always possible. In
some such cases, models can be used to evaluate the means.
Models are representations of reality. They are of three types:

1. Iconic. The properties of the real situation are represented by the same properties but with a change of scale;
   for example, photographs, maps, model ships, pilot plants.

2. **Analogue.** A set of properties that are generally relatively easy to manipulate are used to represent properties of the real situation that are more difficult to manipulate; for example, contour lines on a map used to represent elevation or color to represent topography.

3. **Symbolic.** Symbols are used to represent the properties of the real situation and the relationship between them.

Symbolic models are the most abstract but the easiest to manipulate. They generally take the form of one or more equations, sometimes accompanied by inequations that represent the constraints to which variables in the equation(s) are subject.

In evaluating some means all three types of model are used: iconic and/or analogue models for preliminary approximations and symbolic models for more precise final evaluations. This is similar to the use of a slide rule (an analogue computer) to approximate a calculation that is subsequently carried out precisely using a calculator (a symbolic computer).

A flow diagram of a process often combines iconic and analogue components. Such diagrams are generally qualitative in character but can often be converted into precise quantitative symbolic models.

Models can be used to evaluate means either by experimenting on them (simulation) or, when the model is mathematical, by mathematical analysis or computation. Some symbolic models can be manipulated analytically to determine which combination of values of the controlled variables yields the best, or approximately best, performance. The means found in this way are said to be "optimal." The mathematical procedures by which such means are identified are called "algorithms."

There are some models for which algorithms are not currently available but which can nevertheless be used to compare alternative means that are explicitly formulated. These models can be used to estimate the effectiveness of each means. Then, by using initial comparisons to formulate new alternatives, comparing these, and so on, close approximations to optimal means sometimes can be found.

Any of the three types of model can be used in simulation. When a symbolic model is used, values of variables that are part of the model are sampled and inserted into the model to estimate the outcomes. The distribution of outcomes thus obtained is then used to evaluate means.

Simulation can also be used (1) to study transitional processes, (2) to estimate values of uncontrolled variables, (3) to determine the nature of the relationship between variables, and (4) to treat variables that cannot be represented quantitatively, particularly in the type of simulation called *gaming*. Gaming is simulation in which decisions are made by one or more real decision makers in a simulated environment.

Testing Models

No model, whatever its type, should be used without establishing the accuracy and reliability with which it represents reality. It may fail to do so adequately for any of the following reasons:

1. It omits relevant variables and/or includes ones that are irrelevant.
2. It fails to include a controllable variable.
3. It omits relevant constraints and/or includes ones that are irrelevant.
4. It incorporates an incorrect formulation of the relationship between the variables and the possible outcomes.

The formulation of models is a generalization of the process of formulating alternative means. Therefore, the content of the section on formulation or identification of alternative means is equally applicable to the formulation of models. The controlled variables in a model define the possible means. The model also represents the environment in which they are or will be used, and how changes in any variable, controlled or uncontrolled, affects the outcome.

Models are tested prospectively (against future performance) or retrospectively (against past performance). If a model is tested retrospectively, it is critical that the periods used cover the range of situations that are likely to be encountered in the future.

When a model cannot be tested either prospectively or retrospectively, an analysis of its sensitivity to error can provide some basis for evaluating it. Such an analysis consists of determining by how much the estimates of the values of the variables in the model would have to be in error before the "best" means specified by the model would perform less well than an alternative to it. Then, using judgment as to the likelihood of such critical errors, a partial evaluation of the model can be made.

The Heuristic Use of Models

In addition to their use in evaluating means, models can be used heuristically, that is, to facilitate discovery. They often provide an effective way to explore the assumed structure of a choice situation and to uncover possible courses of action that might otherwise be overlooked.

A detailed discussion of models and their use can be found in Hillier and Lieberman (1980), and Bierman, Bonini, and Hausman (1981).

However means are selected, once selected they constitute a tentative plan of action. The feasibility of such a plan depends on whether the resources required to carry it out will or can be made available. It is to this question that the next phase of planning, resource planning, is addressed.

CHAPTER SIX

Resource Planning

■ ■ ■

Resource planning is directed at determining what resources will be required when and where, and how and where those that will not otherwise be available are to be generated or acquired.

Five types of resource should be taken into account:

1. **Inputs.** Materials, supplies, energy, and services.
2. **Facilities and equipment.** Capital investments.
3. **Personnel.**
4. **Information.**
5. **Money.**

Money can be considered to be a "meta-resource" since its only value lies in its use to obtain other types of resource.

Each of the types of resource required other than money can and should be divided into relevant categories for planning purposes; for example, facilities can be divided into plant, office space, warehouses, and so on. Personnel can be similarly categorized using occupational classes.

The following questions should be asked about inputs, facilities and equipment, and personnel:

1. How much of each type of resource will be required? When and where will it be required?
2. How much of each type of resource will be available at each relevant location at each relevant point in time, assuming no changes in current resource plans or policies?
3. What are the gaps between requirements as determined in step 1 and availabilities as determined in step 2?
4. How should gaps be filled: by developing or generating

them internally or by acquisition from an external source, and how much will filling the gaps cost?

Once these questions have been answered and informational planning (which is discussed below) has been completed, the following questions about money should be addressed:

1. What is the total amount required at each relevant point in time?
2. How much will be available at each relevant point in time?
3. How large are the gaps between 1 and 2?
4. If the required amount of money will not be available, then how can it be obtained and how should previously made planning decisions be modified so as to be able to finance them with funds that will be available? If more than the required amount of money will be available, then how should previously made planning decisions be modified to use all the funds available?

Assignment of responsibility for generating and using money and the schedule for doing so constitute the *budget*.

Now consider each type of resource separately and in more detail.

INPUTS (MATERIALS, SUPPLIES, ENERGY, AND SERVICES)

When calculating input requirements two things should be taken into account. First, their future availability may be in doubt as, for example, the recent case with oil. Second, even if they are available, their expected cost may be so high as to present problems. Potential shortages may be dealt with by any or all of the following:

1. Finding substitutes for the required resource.
2. Integrating vertically.
3. Redesigning products or processes in such a way as to reduce the amount of the resource required.

High costs of inputs may also be dealt with in these ways.

The output of input planning is a set of estimates of the costs of the inputs required per unit time over the period covered by means planning. The assumptions on which these estimates are based should be made explicit so they can be monitored and controlled over time. How this can be done is discussed below.

FACILITIES AND EQUIPMENT

The following questions about facilities and equipment should be addressed:

1. How large should a plant or piece of equipment be?
2. Where should it be located so as to minimize expected costs of transporting inputs to it and outputs from it? (These costs are not the only relevant ones involved in locating a plant, but they are important and may even be overriding.)
3. When should construction or acquisition be initiated?

There are a number of mathematical techniques that are useful for addressing these questions. They can be found in most textbooks on Operations Research (e.g., Hillier and Lieberman, 1980, and Bierman, Bonini, and Hausman, 1981).

Since facility and equipment decisions always depend on estimates of future demand, and since such estimates are frequently in error, it is desirable to hedge against such errors. Flexibility, convertibility, expandability, and contractability are obvious hedges against such uncertainty. These properties involve a cost, but so does their absence. A comparison of these costs is necessary to determine whether requiring such properties of facilities and equipment is justified.

PERSONNEL

The questions that personnel planning should address are:

1. For each year, what is the total number of people in each category that will be required to use the means previously selected?
2. For each year, what is the total number of people expected to be available in each category, given current personnel policies and practices?
3. For each year, what are the gaps between answers to questions 1 and 2?
4. How are the positive gaps to be filled and those that are negative to be treated?

Preparation of the estimates of the number that will be available requires determining the number of employees currently in each category and then estimating their movement in and out of that category (usually) for each year covered by the plan. Movement out of a category may be due to firing, quitting, retirement, promotion, reassignment, or demotion. Therefore, a transition table (Figure 6.1) is required to show the expected movement of personnel from one year to the next. The changes that should be planned for appear in the last column of the table.

INFORMATION

One cannot plan for the acquisition of information in the same way one can for other resources because information differs in a number of ways. For example, it can be duplicated at virtually no cost; it does not decay or wear out, but it may become obsolete or irrelevant; and future requirements for it are virtually impossible to anticipate. Therefore, one cannot determine accurately what will be needed or be available, hence determine what the gaps will be and how to fill them. What is required instead is an information system that will be able to provide whatever information is required.

The design of such systems lies outside the scope of this guide, but there is much readily available information on the subject. (See, for example, McFarlan and McKenney, 1982.)

FINANCIAL PLANNING

Financial planning requires use of a financial model of the organization planned for. Such a model is a set of interconnected equations that can be used for estimating the financial consequences of using different means under the same or different business conditions. There is no single financial model that can represent all corporations or even different parts of the same corporation. Nevertheless, most financial models are similar

Year ——

Personnel category	Number available at beginning of year (a)	Number leaving during year				Number transferred out to				Number transferred in (d)	Number available at end of year (e) = (a − b − c + d)	Number required at end of year (f)	Number to be acquired (+) or moved out (−) (g)=(f − e)
		Fired	Quit	Retired	Total (b)	P_1	P_2	P_n	Total (c)				
P_1						▨				(j)			
P_2							▨			(k)			
$\cdots$								▨		(l)			
P_n								▨		(m)			
Total						(j)	(k)	(l)	(m)	▨			

Figure 6.1
A personnel-requirements planning table.

70

with respect to their essential characteristics. These characteristics are shown schematically in Figure 6.2. The content and flows of a detailed financial model are shown in Figures 6.3a–6.3c. This model was developed for a company whose output consists of multiple brands of one type of consumer product, all using the same production facilities.

Financial models are normally designed to project annual financial reports for five or ten years into the future, but they can be designed for shorter or longer periods. Separate models can also be developed for different geographical areas or types of market and subsequently combined.

The usefulness of financial models is greatly enhanced when they are "computerized." This facilitates rapid financial exploration of a large number of alternative means and/or environmental assumptions. Such explorations obviously have great value in the planning process.

Financial models can be used to estimate the financial consequences of a wide variety of things that might be done under many different business conditions. For example, they can generate projections of such performance measures as:

1. Earnings per share.
2. Dividends per share.
3. Profit per unit sold.
4. Capital availability.
5. Debt to equity ratios.
6. Market share.

Among the types of alternative means that can be evaluated by such models are:

1. Pricing policies.
2. Dividend policies.

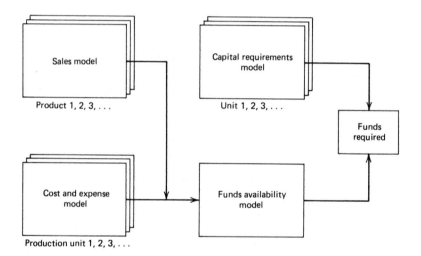

Figure 6.2
Schematic diagram of a financial model.

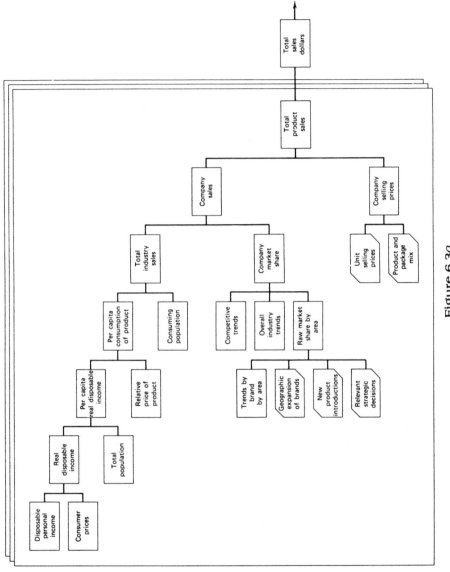

Figure 6.3a
A typical sales submodel.

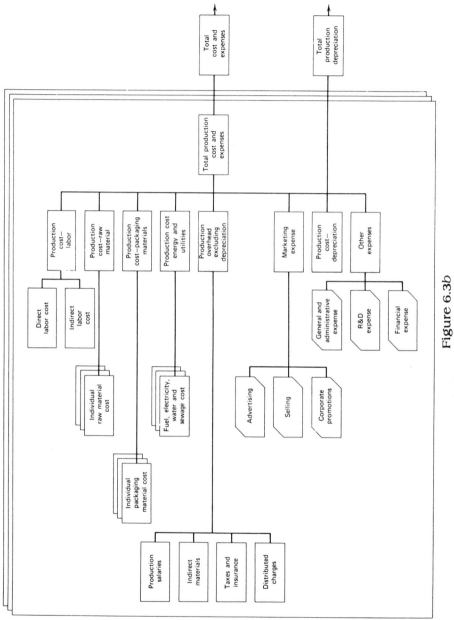

Figure 6.3b

A typical cost-and-expense submodel.

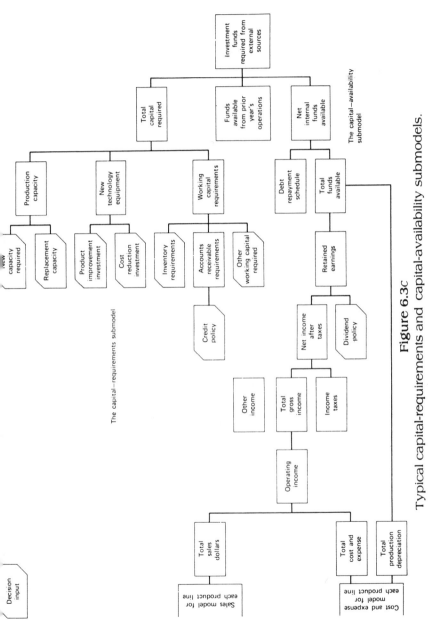

Figure 6.3c

Typical capital-requirements and capital-availability submodels.

3. Borrowing policies.
4. Plant modernization and replacement programs.
5. Process or product modifications.
6. Marketing-mix strategies.

Finally, among the business conditions to which sensitivity can be estimated are:

1. Rate of inflation.
2. Cost of money.
3. Interest rates.

Once means and resources have been brought into balance, implementation and control of the plan can be initiated.

CHAPTER SEVEN

Implementation and Control

■ ■ ■

When the previous phases of planning have been completed, decisions should be made as to who is to be responsible for doing what and by when. Such decisions require the translation of previously made planning decisions into a set of assignments and schedules. These should be worked out with those who are responsible for carrying them out, those to whom they report, and any others who are to be involved.

Implementation planning can be initiated by preparing a PERT-like flow chart of the activities required for the pursuit of each goal and objective. An example of such a chart is shown in Figure 7.1. It is one that was used by a company to organize and schedule the first phase of development of a new food product. The chart identifies the activities required, the time allocated to each, and their timing. If the activities shown in such a chart are to be assigned to more than one individual or unit, those who are to receive such assignments can also be designated on the chart.

The information contained in a PERT-like chart should be combined with that contained in the *Record of Means Selected* (Figure 5.1). This can be done on an *Implementation and Control Form* such as is shown in Figure 7.2. This form should specify:

1. The nature of the task to be carried out.
2. The relevant goal or objective.
3. Who is responsible for carrying it out.
4. The steps to be taken.
5. Who is responsible for each step.
6. The timing of each step.
7. The money allocated to each step, if any.

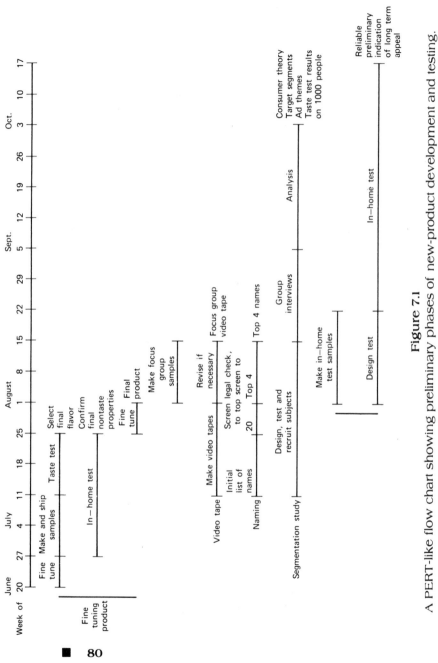

Figure 7.1

A PERT-like flow chart showing preliminary phases of new-product development and testing.

Task:

Goal or objective

Date of issue:

Responsibility of:

Steps	Resposibility of		Percent completed and expenditures Time periods								Comments, explanations and corrective actions
			1		2		. . .		n		
			%	$	%	$	%	$	%	$	
		Planned									
		Actual									
		Planned									
		Actual									
		Planned									
		Actual									
		Planned									
		Actual									
	Total expenditures	Planned									
		Actual									

Assumptions on which implementation schedule is based:

Expected performance and when expected:

Assumptions on which expected performance is based:

Figure 7.2
An example of an implementation and control form.

8. The critical assumptions on which implementation is based.

9. The expected effects on performance and when they are expected.

10. The assumptions on which these expectations are based.

Since each step has two rows beside it, "planned" and "actual," progress can be recorded on this form and compared with the plan. The same type of comparison can be made with respect to expenditures, both by step and time period. The need for corrective action can thus be detected quickly. Explanations of and comments on any significant deviations that have been experienced or are anticipated between "planned" and "actual," as well as corrective actions taken, should be noted in the last column.

For each assumption and expectation that appears on the *Implementation and Control Form* (Figure 7.2), an expanded control form such as is shown in Figure 7.3 should be prepared. These forms can be used to monitor the control process. They indicate what is to be monitored, by whom, when, the results of each check, explanations of deviations when available, and the corrective actions taken.

When assumed and actual conditions, or expected and actual performance, agree, nothing need be done. When they disagree, an effort should be made to determine what has gone wrong or unexpectedly right. Although the producers of unfavorable deviations may be difficult to identify, there are only four types:

1. The information used in selecting the means was in error. If this is the case, a change of the information source should be prescribed, one that will prevent repetition of the same type of error.

2. The means-selection process was faulty. In such a case, a change in the process is in order.

Assumption/expectation to be checked:

Task to which related:

Who is responsible for making check:

Time of Check	Results	Explanation of Deviation	Corrective Action Taken
1.			
2.			
• • • n.			

Figure 7.3
Assumption/expectation control form.

3. The implementation was not carried out as intended. If this is the case, changes are required to improve either the communications from the decision makers to those responsible for implementation, or the behavior of those who are responsible for it.

4. The environment changed in a way that was not anticipated. In these cases, either a better way of anticipating such changes, decreasing sensitivity to them, or reducing their likelihood should be found. Doing so may require any one or more of the three types of change mentioned above, or efforts to change the environment.

The effective conduct of such diagnoses and prescriptions can assure both effective learning and adaptation. Without these, effective continuous planning is not possible. Without such planning, continuous progress towards organizational objectives, let alone ideals, is not possible. Without a sense of progress towards ideals, the quality of working life deteriorates. With such deterioration, work loses its meaning and becomes drudgery.

CHAPTER EIGHT

Reference
Scenarios

■ ■ ■

SCENARIO 1

The following reference scenario was prepared early in 1979. It involved the large multiplant operation of a corporation. For some time this operation, located in "Greensville," had been experiencing decreasing productivity and quality of output, and increasing conflict between management and labor. Corporate headquarters had recently decided to shut down most of the operation and had set a date by which this was to be done. The reference projections revealed that the parts of the operation to be terminated were not likely to last even until that date if its then current trends were to continue.

The scenario was written in the form of a feature article in the local press. This "article," together with the other outputs of the formulation of the mess, succeeded in focusing the subsequent planning effort on labor–management relations. A collaborative effort of management and the union was initiated and eventually produced a complete turnaround of the operation. The corporation subsequently revoked its decision to terminate the operation.

In this scenario, as in all the final chapters, we have made minor changes in the original documents in order to protect the organizations involved.

■ ■ ■

From the *Greensville Times*, April 10, 1984, p. 1:

GREEN COUNTY TO LOSE ALPHA PLANT AND 2,300 JOBS

Economic disaster hit the Greensville area yesterday. The Alpha Corporation announced that in October of this year it was going to close two of its three plants operating in Greensville. Workers at all three plants have been on strike for the last six weeks.

The full impact of the closing will not be felt for months, but the severity of it was apparent yesterday. Alpha paid $1,300,000 in property taxes last year. This made up 60 percent of Greensville's income. The corporation currently spends about $400, 000,000 per year in this area.

"It's certainly a shock," said Greensville's Mayor Jones. He also said that he and other local officials had become concerned by recent layoffs and job reduction in Alpha's local operation. Its work force has been reduced from 4,600 to 3,600 in the last two years. The Mayor pointed out that he had requested, but had not been granted, a meeting with Alpha's executives to discuss ways by which he and the community might help keep the plants open.

Mayor Jones said that Alpha's Greensville operation was the largest employer in the area and for years it has paid its production workers considerably more than other industrial employers in the area. When asked about the effect of the closing on Greensville, the Mayor said major cutbacks in public services and consolidation and closing of several schools were likely.

A spokesman for Alpha denied that the closing is related to the six-week-old strike at the Greensville operation. He attributed the closing to the weak national economy and recent restrictive measures of the federal government. He also said that increasing energy costs and material shortages contributed to the decision to close. "The cost of energy per unit of output has increased by 200 percent in the past four years." In the last few years the company has shifted many of its operations overseas to countries in which labor and energy costs are much lower than they are in the United States.

Joe Smith, President of Local 100 of the union to which all hourly workers in Alpha's Greensville operation belong, said, "I don't believe Alpha is serious about this closing. In 1967 they threatened to do the same thing and didn't. If they think they are going to break the strike by this announcement, they'd better think again."

Yesterday, when the striking workers received word of the intended closing, about 1,000 of them stormed the plants and vowed not to leave until the company meets their demands and rescinds the closing order.

As recently as January, officials of Alpha's Greensville operation told the Times that they did not foresee additional layoffs beyond the 400 that took place at the end of last year. "We are looking for increases in employment when conditions get better," they had said.

William Brown, general manager of Alpha's local operation, would not elaborate on his prepared statement that expressed his regret at the closing and his intention to help workers affected by it find other employment. He said that 600 white-collar and 1,700 blue-collar workers would be let go. When asked whether the company had considered what it would eventually do with the two plants to be closed, he had no comment. He did say that the company is currently seeking an injunction to remove the strikers from the plant.

Just last week, Alpha reported a $10,000,000 loss in the first quarter of this year. This was attributed in part to the current protracted strike. However, an informed source said that Alpha's Greensville operation has been in trouble for a long time. Management and the union have been unable to work together on problems of productivity and quality. Their distrust of each other has reduced the operation's ability to compete effectively. For this reason, he said, the corporation has invested very little in maintenance of the Greensville plants, and even less in their modernization. He also said that recent setbacks in Alpha's overseas operations, including nationalization of two of its plants in Latin American countries, have severely limited the corporation's ability to sustain unprofitable operations like those in Greensville.

One of Alpha's three plants in this area will remain open. It employs approximately 1,250.

SCENARIO 2

The following reference scenario of the trucking industry was prepared in 1980 for one of its major suppliers. It consists of a set of reference projections of the environment of the company involved. Projections applicable to the company itself are not included.

This rather gloomy extrapolated future of the trucking industry has not been contradicted in the two years that have passed since it was prepared. If anything, the extrapolated future looks even more gloomy. Although the fuel situation has improved, the "foreign invasion" is greater than was projected. The continuing generally poor state of the national economy has significantly depressed the industry. The need for diversification that was indicated by the scenario is at least as pressing today as it was when these projections were made.

■ ■ ■

Number of Trucks

Since 1960 the number of trucks of all kinds has been increasing at an annual rate of a little less than one million (Table 8.1).

However, the number of personal trucks has been increasing at slightly more than this rate. If these two trends were to continue, the number of trucks used for handling freight would decrease slightly over the next twenty years. This does not make for a growth industry.

The number of trucks for hire has declined substantially over the last fourteen years: from 804,921 in 1963 to 709,500 in 1977, indicating a significant shift to use of privately owned trucks for hauling freight (Table 8.1). Use of trucks by manufacturing industries has been decreasing but is increasing in all other industrial categories.

Based on data from 1963, 1967, 1972, and 1977, the projections for the total number of trucks on the road (classified as "personal" and "nonpersonal") to the year 2000 is given in Table 8.2.

The percentage of all trucks replaced per year from 1947 to 1978 has varied between 3.7 and 9.0 with an average of 6.1. Assuming no significant change in these rates, the number of nonpersonal trucks to be replaced over the next twenty years is given in Table 8.3. In summary, these numbers are:

	1981	2000
Pessimistic	532,398	692,091
Average	881,784	1,146,276
Optimistic	1,295,022	1,683,464

Hard data on the current domestic production capacity for nonpersonal trucks are not available, but it was estimated very conservatively as follows. Over the past ten years the maximum number of trucks that each manufacturer produced in any one year was determined, and these were summed (Table 8.4). The estimate of capacity obtained in this way was 3,739,174. This figure was divided between personal and nonpersonal trucks in the same proportion as the total number of trucks in 1977 (29,562,485) was broken down into personal trucks (16,081,992)

Table 8.1
Total Number of Trucks

Year	Total	Personal	For-Hire	Manufacturing	Other	Nonpersonal
1963	13,642,730	3,342,469	804,921	627,566	8,867,774	10,300,261
1967	16,376,399	5,502,470	720,562	393,034	9,760,333	10,873,929
1972	21,559,339	8,882,448	840,814	495,865	11,340,212	12,676,891
1977	29,562,485	16,081,992	709,500	413,875	12,357,118	13,480,493

Sources: Truck Inventory and Use Survey, U.S. Bureau of the Census, 1963, 1967, 1972, and 1977.

Table 8.2
Total Number of Trucks on the Road

Year	Total	Personal	Nonpersonal
1963	13,642,730	3,342,469	10,300,261
1977	29,562,485	16,081,992	13,480,493
1978	30,699,610	16,991,958	13,707,652
1979	31,836,736	17,901,924	13,934,812
1980	32,973,861	18,811,890	14,161,971
1981	34,110,986	19,721,856	14,389,131
1982	35,248,112	20,631,822	14,616,290
1983	36,385,237	21,541,788	14,843,450
1984	37,522,363	22,451,754	15,070,609
1985	38,659,488	23,361,719	15,297,768
1986	39,796,613	24,271,685	15,524,928
1987	40,933,739	25,181,651	15,752,087
1988	42,070,864	26,091,617	15,979,247
1989	43,207,989	27,001,583	16,206,406
1990	44,345,115	27,911,549	16,433,566
1991	45,482,240	28,821,515	16,660,725
1992	46,619,365	29,731,481	16,887,884
1993	47,756,491	30,641,447	17,115,044
1994	48,893,616	31,551,413	17,342,203
1995	50,030,741	32,461,379	17,569,363
1996	51,167,867	33,371,345	17,796,522
1997	52,304,992	34,281,311	18,023,682
1998	53,442,118	35,191,277	18,250,841
1999	54,579,243	36,101,242	18,478,000
2000	55,716,368	37,011,208	18,705,160

Table 8.3
Projected Number of New Nonpersonal
Trucks Required

Year	Total	Pessimistic	Average	Optimistic
1981	14,389,131	532,398	881,784	1,295,022
1982	14,616,290	540,803	895,705	1,315,466
1983	14,843,450	549,208	909,625	1,335,910
1984	15,070,609	557,613	923,546	1,356,355
1985	15,297,768	566,017	937,466	1,376,799
1986	15,524,928	574,422	951,387	1,397,244
1987	15,752,087	582,827	965,308	1,417,688
1988	15,979,247	591,232	979,228	1,438,132
1989	16,206,406	599,637	993,149	1,458,577
1990	16,433,566	608,042	1,007,069	1,479,021
1991	16,660,725	616,447	1,020,990	1,499,465
1992	16,887,884	624,852	1,034,911	1,519,910
1993	17,115,044	633,257	1,048,831	1,540,354
1994	17,342,203	641,662	1,062,752	1,560,798
1995	17,569,363	650,066	1,076,673	1,581,243
1996	17,796,522	658,471	1,090,593	1,601,687
1997	18,023,682	666,876	1,104,514	1,622,131
1998	18,250,841	675,281	1,118,434	1,642,576
1999	18,478,000	683,686	1,132,355	1,663,020
2000	18,705,160	692,091	1,146,276	1,683,464

and nonpersonal trucks (13,480,493). This led to an estimate of 46 percent for nonpersonal trucks. Therefore, the estimate of the domestic capacity for production of nonpersonal trucks was 46 percent of at least 3,739,174, which is 1,720,020.

Table 8.5 gives the projected number of replacement trucks required (for each of the three replacement ratios given above), expressed as a percentage of 1,720,020, the estimated domestic capacity for producing nonpersonal trucks. The following is a summary of it:

Table 8.4
Maximum Domestic Production

Manufacturer	Total	Year
Chevrolet	1,122,769	(1977)
Dodge	489,164	(1978)
Ford	1,233,122	(1978)
International	212,654	(1972)
Jeep	180,514	(1978)
Mack	35,937	(1979)
White	31,518	(1978)
Others	58,436	(1978)
TOTAL	3,739,174	

	1981	2000
Pessimistic	30.95%	40.24%
Average	51.27	66.64
Optimistic	75.29	97.87

These very conservatively estimated figures suggest that a number of current manufacturers of nonpersonal trucks may be forced out of business. The pressure to do so could be significantly increased by more importation of truck tractors. We have no accurate estimate of what this might be, but if we assume a 10 percent share for foreign tractors in 2000, then the percent of capacity required (cited above) reduces to:

	1981	2000
Pessimistic	30.95%	36.22%
Average	51.27	59.98
Optimistic	75.29	88.08

Table 8.5
Projected Number of New Nonpersonal
Trucks Required
(As a percentage of maximum capacity of 1,720,020)

Year	Total	Pessimistic	Average	Optimistic
1981	14,389,131	30.95	51.27	75.29
1982	14,616,290	31.44	52.08	76.48
1983	14,843,450	31.93	52.88	77.67
1984	15,070,609	32.42	53.69	78.86
1985	15,297,768	32.91	54.50	80.05
1986	15,524,928	33.40	55.31	81.23
1987	15,752,087	33.88	56.12	82.42
1988	15,979,247	34.37	56.93	83.61
1989	16,206,406	34.86	57.74	84.80
1990	16,433,566	35.35	58.55	85.99
1991	16,660,725	35.84	59.36	87.18
1992	16,887,884	36.33	60.17	88.37
1993	17,115,044	36.82	60.98	89.55
1994	17,342,203	37.31	61.79	90.74
1995	17,569,363	37.79	62.60	91.93
1996	17,796,522	38.28	63.41	93.12
1997	18,023,682	38.77	64.22	94.31
1998	18,250,841	39.26	65.02	95.50
1999	18,478,000	39.75	65.83	96.69
2000	18,705,160	40.24	66.64	97.87

Fuel

From 1963 to 1977 the ratio of gasoline-fueled to diesel- and LPG- fueled trucks has decreased from 46.2 (13,247,091/286,497) to 24.6 (28,379,986/1,152,937). On the other hand, in 1967 the ratio was 7.9 (Table 8.6). There is no clear trend. Therefore, the future is likely to depend critically on relative fuel prices. Diesel fuel increased at a slightly higher rate from 1975 to 1979 than did gasoline: 26 percent as compared to 18.5 percent. Currently,

Table 8.6
Estimated Number of Trucks by Fuel Type

Type	1963	1967	1972	1977
Gasoline	13,247,091	14,116,456	18,950,659	28,379,986
Diesel and LPG	286,497	1,785,027	948,611	1,152,937

Source: Truck Inventory and Use Survey, U.S. Bureau of the Census, 1963, 1967, 1972, and 1977.

diesel fuel costs about 2.1 times as much as it did five years ago, but gasoline costs 1.9 times as much (Table 8.7). Therefore, there is no strong indication that the percentage of diesel- and LPG-fueled trucks will increase and, because of the trend in fuel prices, it may decrease.

Table 8.7
Retail Fuel Expense

Year	Quarter	Avg. Price/Gallon		Avg. Price/Gallon	
		Diesel	Index	Reg. Gas	Index
1975	4th	51.9¢	100.0	60.7¢	100.0
1976	1st	52.2	100.6	59.7	98.4
	2nd	52.2	100.6	59.8	98.5
	3rd	53.1	102.3	62.0	102.1
	4th	53.9	103.9	62.4	102.8
1977	1st	56.6	109.1	62.7	103.3
	2nd	57.9	111.6	64.3	105.9
	3rd	58.5	112.7	65.1	107.3
	4th	58.8	113.3	64.7	106.6
1978	1st	59.3	114.3	64.7	106.6
	2nd	59.5	114.6	65.0	107.1
	3rd	59.8	115.2	66.8	110.1
	4th	61.1	117.7	68.4	112.7
1979	1st	65.4	126.0	71.9	118.5

Source: Household Goods Carriers' Bureau data base.

The estimated number of miles per gallon of trucks has been relatively stable at about 8.45 for thirty years (Table 8.8). The total amount of fuel consumed per truck per year has also been relatively constant at about 1,325 gallons. With the added number of both personal and nonpersonal trucks projected, an additional 26,153,883 vehicles and 34,654 million gallons of motor fuel would be used. This would be a 32 percent increase in fuel consumption. Such an increase would create a major national problem unless there are significant changes in the fuel-supply situation. If there is a shortage of fuel, freight-hauling trucks are likely to receive preferential treatment but, perhaps of greater importance, it is likely that regulations that currently increase fuel consumption will be relaxed. For example, the use of several trailers behind a tractor may be more generally permitted. If such action were taken, there would be fewer but larger trucks in use.

Highways

The number of intercity miles traveled by trucks has increased over the last twenty years by about 100 million miles, or 5 million miles per year (Figure 8.1). A similar increase over the next twenty years would be about a 50 percent increase. Most of this would come from personal trucks.

Annual expenditure on intercity highways has increased by about $26.5 billion over the last twenty years, a 200 percent increase (Table 8.9). If this rate of expenditure were to continue, there would be no problem created by the increase in the number of trucks projected. Although congestion caused by trucks between cities does not seem likely to present a problem, congestion caused by automobiles may.

The projected intracity picture is not as reassuring. Intracity truck mileage has increased by about 175 million miles in the last twenty years, or 3.5 times. Most cities, of course, are al-

Table 8.8
Motor Fuel Consumption, by Use, 1950–1975[a]

Item	1950	1955	1960	1965	1970	1971	1972	1973	1974	1975
Total consumption[b] (bil. gal)	40.3	53.1	63.7	71.1	92.3	97.6	105.1	110.5	106.3	109.0
Avg. annual change (%)	12.5[c]	5.7	3.7	2.2	5.4	5.7	7.7	5.2	−3.8	2.5
Passenger vehicles (bil. gal)	25.0	34.3	42.0	51.2	66.7	70.5	74.3	78.9	75.1	77.4
Cars[d] (bil. gal)	24.3	33.5	41.2	50.3	65.8	69.5	73.5	78.0	74.2	76.5
Buses (incl. school) (bil. gal)	.7	.8	.8	.9	.9	.9	.9	.8	.9	.9
Trucks[e] (bil. gal)	10.6	13.3	15.9	19.9	25.6	27.1	30.7	31.6	31.2	31.6
Average gallons per vehicle										
Cars[d]	728	759	777	775	830	838	859	851	788	790
Buses (incl. school)	603	644	661	656	722	723	730	736	676	685
Trucks[e]	3,752	3,021	3,040	2,844	2,491	2,382	2,165	1,991	1,919	1,937
	1,257	1,278	1,330	1,347	1,365	1,368	1,446	1,361	1,268	1,227
Average mileage per gallon										
Cars[d]	12.87	12.67	12.42	12.49	12.14	12.16	12.07	11.85	12.09	12.20
Buses (incl. school)	14.95	14.53	14.28	14.15	13.58	13.73	13.67	13.29	13.65	13.74
Trucks[e]	5.57	5.85	5.26	5.35	5.34	5.38	5.80	5.86	5.90	5.75
	8.57	8.37	7.96	8.60	8.39	8.38	8.59	8.45	8.57	8.68

Source: *Statistical Abstract of the United States, 1977*, U.S. Department of Commerce, Bureau of the Census, Washington, D.C. (From U.S. Federal Highway Administration, *Highway Statistics*, annual.)

[a]Prior to 1960, excludes Alaska and Hawaii. Comprises all fuels (gas, diesel, or other fuels used for propulsion of vehicles) under state motor fuels laws. Excludes exports and Federal purchases for military use. See also *Historical Statistics, Colonial Times to 1970*, series Q 156-162.
[b]Through 1960, includes nonhighway usage and losses allowed for evaporation, handling, etc.; thereafter, highway usage only.
[c]Change from 1945.
[d]Includes taxicabs and motorcycles.
[e]Includes combinations.

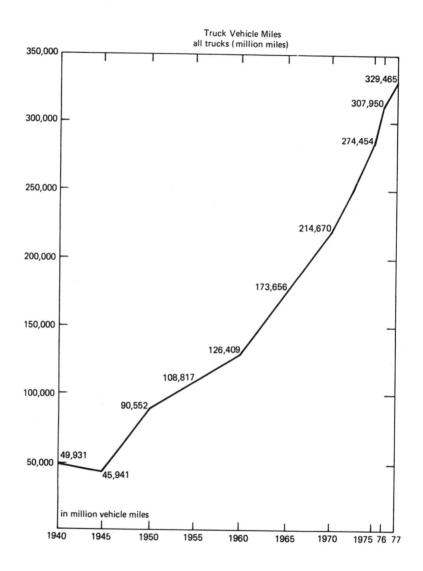

Figure 8.1

Travel Total
million miles

	Main and Local Rural Roads	Urban Streets	Travel Total
1940	30,207	19,724	49,931
1945	27,181	18,760	45,941
1950	56,780	33,772	90,552
1955	69,096	39,721	108,817
1960[1]	81,722	44,687	126,409
1965	108,500	65,057	173,656
1970	134,064	80,606	214,670
1973	153,180	113,154	267.147
1974	156,775	114,339	267,519
1975	163,073	117,679	274,454
1976r	176,115	144,877	307,950
1977e	19,774	153,350	329,465

*Series revised after 1955.
e—Estimated ATA Department of Research and Statistical Services.
r—Revised.
SOURCE: U. S. Department of Transportation Federal Highway Administration

Figure 8.1 (Continued)

Table 8.9
Federal and State Expenditures for Highways
(In millions of dollars)

Year	Expender	Amount	Total
1947	Federal	337	
	State and local	2,529	2,866
1950	Federal	503	
	State and local	3,652	4,155
1955	Federal	784	
	State and local	6,157	6,941
1960	Federal	2,753	
	State and local	7,407	10,160
1965	Federal	4,137	
	State and local	9,319	13,456
1970	Federal	5,181	
	State and local	14,321	19,502
1975	Federal	7,180r	
	State and local	20,027r	27,207r
1976	Federal	7,939	
	State and local	20,309	28,248
1977	Federal	8,079p	
	State and local	21,294p	29,373p

Source: Transportation Association of America, Transportation Facts and Trends, Washington, D.C., 1980.
Key: r-revised; p-preliminary.

ready heavily congested and cannot absorb such an increase in truck traffic. Therefore, regulations that constrain the use of trucks to specified times or restrict the types of trucks that can be used within cities are quite likely.

Summary
Assuming no changes in current trends, the trucking industry does not appear to have prospects for significant growth. The

foreign invasion is likely to reduce the number of American trucks purchased. These two trends, in combination, would put several tractor and trailer manufacturers out of business, concentrating what remains in a few large cost-efficient and technologically innovative manufacturers.

Tractors are likely to become larger and more powerful to pull larger loads between cities, and innovation to reduce fuel consumption is quite likely.

Use of tractors and trailers within cities is likely to be more restricted than it is currently, but use between cities is likely to be less restricted with larger loads permitted in order to conserve fuel.

CHAPTER NINE

Mission
Statements

The following mission statements were prepared by very different organizations:

1. A subsidiary of a large Mexican corporation.
2. A group of CEOs active in a major city's Chamber of Commerce who came together to find a way to contribute more effectively to their city's development.
3. Employees at all levels of a major supermarket chain who came together to design and implement a new subsidiary chain of stores.
4. A research organization engaged to study the trucking system of the United States.

MISSION 1

The general mission proposed for Beta is:

Through land development and tourism, to demonstrate the ability of the private sector of the Mexican economy to contribute significantly to national development while efficiently and effectively pursuing corporate objectives.

The specific mission proposed for Beta in the target area is:

To create a wholesome, varied, pluralistic, multiclass recreational area incorporating tourist facilities and permanent residences and to produce locally as much of the goods and services required by the area as possible, so as to improve the standards of living and the quality of life of its inhabitants.

MISSION 2

The mission of the long-range planning committee of the Gamma Chamber of Commerce is:

> *To organize the Gamma Chamber of Commerce and its members so they can more effectively provide the leadership necessary to promote economic development by creating an environment and quality of life that will encourage and facilitate:*
> 1. *The formation of new businesses.*
> 2. *The retention of old ones.*
> 3. *The attraction of businesses from outside.*
> 4. *The growth of all of these.*

To this end the committee proposes to consolidate and coordinate the efforts and activities of the area's business community to play a vital role in the development of the area through its own activities, and through collaboration with government, non-business groups, and other organizations.

MISSION 3

To create a viable shopping environment that provides the customer with a consistent and satisfying shopping experience on a day-to-day basis.

To do this effectively Delta will pursue the following three interrelated objectives:

1. Provide a quality product; a courteous, pleasant, and helpful shopping environment; and a pricing structure which represents value to the customer.

2. Create a unique, positive experience for employees to increase their quality of working life through helping design their future as employees and the future of the company.

3. Generate a new model that demonstrates a successful and profitable operation of a volume-oriented business.

Delta will create a new working style and environment for the food retail business that will encourage a quality of working life where the employees have the desire and the ability to improve themselves as well as the business they are in. This environment will be enhanced by opportunities for employees: participation in an investment/incentive fund; participation in decisions that affect them; to continuously learn and grow in their jobs. This will give them a sense of ownership not only in the individual store but in the company as a whole. Delta and the Unions will have a relationship that is trusting and cooperative so that they work together for the benefit of each other. Delta will be recognized within the food-retailing industry and within each community it serves as the model which others try to emulate. At the same time Delta will, by its performance, redefine upwardly the industry's standard of profit.

MISSION 4

We take the mission of the trucking system to be to provide truck transport of goods in a commercial context, as part of an integrated national multimodal transportation system, in such a way as to satisfy:

1. *Public* interests by (a) contributing minimally to environmental pollution (including noise), congestion, and acci-

dents, (b) using as little energy as possible, (c) wearing roads as little as possible, and (d) being aesthetically inoffensive, if not pleasing.

2. *User* desires for inexpensive, fast, reliable, predictable, safe, and easily accessible transportation of goods.

3. The desires of *those who work in the system* for adequate and fair compensation, safety, and a satisfying quality of working life.

4. *Those who produce the equipment* used in the system with continuing, if not expanding, sources of business, and with incentives to improve their equipment and its use through research and development.

5. *Those who own and operate transportation services* by providing them with equipment that is flexible, reliable, easy to maintain, safe, energy-conserving, economical to operate, and reasonably priced.

CHAPTER TEN

Specification
of Desired
Properties

The first of the following two sets of specifications was prepared by the same team of employees that formulated the third mission statement in Chapter 9 for a new subsidiary chain of supermarkets.

The second was formulated by employees, also at all levels, of an insurance company.

SPECIFICATIONS 1

1. General

1.1. The organizational design will be based on the criteria of incorporating the advantages of operating an individual supermarket along with the advantages of the synergistic effects of combining the stores into a corporation.

1.2. The organization will operate with as few managements levels as possible.

1.3. Decision making will be at the lowest possible level where participation will be reflected by authority and responsibility.

1.4. The employees, called associates, will have access to information about their work and the corporation which will allow for meaningful input to decisions.

1.5. The organization will be capable of functional flexibility. Emphasis will be placed on organizational learning and adaptability.

1.6. The relationship between Delta and the union will be cooperative; they will assist each other in obtaining mutual objectives.

1.7. The organization is to be so constructed that it is assured of being economically viable, technologically feasible, able to adapt to the changing needs of its environment and its members, and able to encourage a quality of working life where the associates have both the *desire* and the *ability* to improve themselves and the company with which they are associated.

1.8. Each store is the output unit of Delta and can be viewed as a subsidiary of Delta, using the services provided by the company to its advantage. The individual store's performance will be measured by three factors: gross sales, labor ratio (percentage of gross sales), and contribution to Delta (dollars and percentage of sales).

1.9. The image of Delta should reflect, among other things, the unique organizational design involving the cooperation of associates, union, and management.

2. Output

Delta will constantly pursue the following objectives: loyal customers, satisfied employees, and adequate return on investment.

2.1. Products. A good selection of prepackaged, processed, and prepared products should be provided.

(a) Items offered for sale by each store will be tailored to the customers' needs within each community served by a store.

(b) Stores will strive to develop a one-step food service for their customers.

(c) Stores will not be limited to food items and may sell nonfood items as well.

2.2. Services. There will be a variety of convenience services available for customers. These will include among others: check cashing, customer service center, customer special orders, and customer education.

3. Processes

The following processes will transform inputs to outputs.

3.1. The following processes will be performed by the organization at the corporate level:

(a) Employee development.

(b) Financial planning and control, including asset control, capital investment, etc.

(c) Human resources management.

(d) Procurement and distribution.

(e) Marketing.

(f) Policy setting.

(g) Performance monitoring.

(h) Store selection and property management.

(i) Union/management relationship (including collective bargaining).

3.2. The following processes will be performed by the organization at the store level:

(a) Each department should manage its own proccesses, such as selecting, ordering, storing, displaying.

(b)   Customer handling and relations.

(c)   Cleaning.

(d)   Scheduling/development.

(e)   Risk management.

(f)   Human resources management.

(g)   Cash and asset control.

(h)   Union/store management/associate relationships (grievances).

(i)   Community relationships.

4. Input

4.1.   Money. The capital investment will be provided by banks. Delta will generate the working capital needed for the successful operation of the business. Banks will be asked to assist in obtaining credit whenever the need arises. The president of Delta will negotiate to retain a percentage of the profit for reinvestment in the company; for example, for modernization and expansion.

4.2.   Knowledge. Associates will be taught to be proficient in their jobs and will also be exposed to the total supermarket operation. The knowledge requirement of the company will be principally provided internally by the associates.

4.3.   People. Personnel will be selected to facilitate the attainment of the Delta mission.

4.4.   Facilities. Facilities for the stores will be designed to suit specific locations. Equipment for the stores will be standardized for easier maintenance and modification.

4.5. Inventory. Delta will obtain inventory on a competitive basis.

5. Environment

Delta will create working relationships with the following stakeholders:

(a) Associates.
(b) Customers.
(c) Community at large.
(d) Unions.
(e) Suppliers.
(f) Creditors.
(g) Service vendors.
(h) Former employees.

SPECIFICATIONS 2

1. Business Form

1.1. The enterprise should have mutual component(s).

1.2. The enterprise should have stock component(s) to provide additional flexibility to offer a broad line of products and services and enhance its tax-planning capabilities.

1.3. In addition to ownership affiliations there should be

provisions for entering into business relationships with other organizations.

1.4.   The enterprise should remain flexible in order to take advantage of a changing environment.

1.5.   The enterprise will comply with all laws and regulations of the jurisdictions in which it operates, but will seek to change or modify in appropriate ways those that obstruct its development.

2.   Board of Directors

The board of the parent should bring to the enterprise fresh and innovative viewpoints and relevant competencies not available in the company. Its membership should include some who are actively involved in corporate management. Only individuals who can make a significant contribution to the success of the enterprise would be chosen.

3.   Markets

3.1.   The enterprise's market should be

(a)   Upper- and upper-middle-income individuals.

(b)   Other individuals where they are upwardly mobile, or where serving them aids in attracting and developing new agents or provides a particularly attractive profit opportunity.

(c)   Medium to small businesses and other organizations, and their employees.

3.2.   Other markets would be identified for other financial services and ancillary operations, such as specialized investment services for pension plans of large corporations.

3.3. Although these are ideal markets at the present time, the enterprise should periodically review its strengths and weaknesses to determine whether these choices remain most appropriate. Furthermore, the enterprise should periodically review its effectiveness in those market segments within which it operates.

3.4. The enterprise should focus on the United States, but could consider international markets.

3.5. Within broadly defined markets which the enterprise addresses there should be a mechanism to select the most attractive segments and concentrate on those chosen segments.
The enterprise should have a mechanism to determine consumer needs within its chosen market segments and respond to those needs.

3.6. The resources and benefits associated with the enterprise's selected market segments should be measurable and/or capable of explicit definition so that the ultimate profitability to the enterprise of each market segment could be measured.

4. Products and Services

4.1. The enterprise should produce or procure highly competitive products and services capable of meeting selected financial needs of consumers in identified market segments.
The enterprise should continuously engage in market research and environmental surveillance to identify existing and emerging needs of consumers in the selected market segments.

The enterprise should be prepared to act expeditiously on those products and services which show the greatest potential with respect to existing and emerging needs and be prepared to discontinue those that have failed to meet expectations.

Such products and services should be made available to clients from sources either within or outside the enterprise.

4.2. The product mix should be diverse to minimize the impact on the enterprise of uncontrollable external events, such as economic cycles.

4.3. Each product or service should be demonstrably profitable to the enterprise in the long run either by itself or in combination with other specific products or services.

The resources and benefits associated with the product or service should be measurable or, if intangible, capable of explicit definition so that the performances of the product or service can be measured and compared to expectations.

4.4. Changes in products or services must enhance the long-run viability of the total enterprise.

5. Distribution

5.1. The enterprise should have wide distribution capabilities and the capacity for multiple distribution systems.

5.2. The enterprise's distributors should have the capacity to offer a broad range of products and services, including those produced by other organizations, within parameters established by the enterprise.

5.3. Each distribution system, or element thereof, should be self-supporting in the sense that its net contribution to profits should be reasonable in relation to that achievable from any alternative system. Up-front investment needed to establish a distribution system, or element thereof, should be related to profit potential and likelihood of success.

5.4. The marketing outlets should focus primarily on sales and client contacts rather than administrative and servicing functions.

6. Organization Structure

6.1. At the top level there are two distinct functions: one which deals with enterprise strategy, public affairs and industry matters; and one which deals with directing enterprise operations.

6.2. The enterprise should be organized to facilitate efficient operations, to allow rapid response to changing conditions, to clearly define accountabilities and responsibilities, and to provide incentives to perform in the best interests of the enterprise.

The organization should provide for policy setting at the top and decision making at the lowest possible level.

Members of the enterprise should have access to the resources needed to carry out their responsibilities and should be accountable for their decisions.

Each unit in the enterprise should be managed so as to accomplish specific measurable goals as stipulated at the enterprise level.

6.3. Subsidiary companies should be an integral part of

the enterprise and should have competitive access
to enterprise resources.

Some subsidiaries should be able to achieve greater
independence as they grow and become viable enti-
ties which do not need to depend entirely upon the
parent for resources.

Other subsidiaries, depending upon their purpose,
may be operated in such a manner as to be wholly or
mainly dependent upon the parent for resources.

7. Human Resources

7.1. A primary objective of the enterprise should be the
      personal and professional development of its people
      and the productive use of their capabilities.

7.2. The enterprise should take advantage of technological
      advances to increase productivity.

7.3. The enterprise should provide an environment that
      enhances the use and growth of individuals' talents.

7.4. Enterprise personnel should be evaluated and re-
      warded on the basis of their performance and should
      be provided incentives for superior results.

7.5. The enterprise should encourage its personnel to
      continue their education in their specialities and in
      the enterprise's industry.

7.6. The enterprise should take advantage of other re-
      sources available outside the enterprise by utilizing
      outside consultants and cooperative ventures where
      this would aid efficient and effective operations.

CHAPTER ELEVEN

Idealized Designs

■ ■ ■

Three idealized designs are presented in this chapter.

The first was prepared by the employees at the same operation whose reference scenario is in Chapter 8 (Scenario 1). Only a portion of their design is presented here because of the great length of the original. The design as a whole has been systematically approximated since its preparation.

The second design was prepared by the research group that prepared Reference Scenario 2 of the trucking industry. This design is being used by one truck manufacturer in the preparation of a strategic plan.

The third design was prepared by the externally acquired staff of a committee of major league baseball club owners formed in 1981 to consider the reorganization of the game. The design presented here was subsequently modified considerably by the committee and submitted to the Board of Baseball where it is currently being discussed.

IDEALIZED DESIGN 1

The Social System

The people-related objectives of the sociotechnical system called Alpha are:

1. To provide all employees with a high quality of work life, stable employment, satisfying work, and equal opportunity for advancement.
2. To create a homogeneous work force in which employees

of different race, religion, sex, and national origin experience no discrimination or segregation; and which is dedicated to turning out high-quality products as efficiently as they can.

3. To encourage and facilitate the personal development of each employee.

The principles of design by means of which these objectives are sought are:

1. To locate decision making at the lowest level at which all the information required is available, and to provide those with such responsibility with the resources necessary for implementing their decisions.

2. To develop collaboratively with all employees explicit measures of their performance and to provide them with periodic feedback on it to enable them to learn and adapt rapidly and effectively.

3. To provide all those who are directly affected by a decision with an opportunity to participate in making it.

Organization

Introduction

1. Alpha will be organized with no more than five levels of supervision (operations manager, department manager, superintendent, area or shift supervisor, and unit supervisor).

   1.1. Each level of the organization will have the following five dimensions:

   (a) *Outputs.* Output units produce goods or services

that result in income to the organization from external sources.

(b) *Inputs and services.* Input and service units supply the organization with needed services and inputs that are necessary to carry out their responsibility.

(c) *Development and advocacy.* Development and advocacy units are responsible for providing the impetus for change at Alpha based on internal and external stimuli.

(d) *Planning.* Planning will be done by a planning board which on each level represents the participative ongoing process of interactive planning.

(e) *Management control systems.* The management control system monitors the day-to-day ongoing operation of Alpha and measures and observes the effect of decisions of the planning board.

Outputs

2. The first level will have the following semiautonomous output units:

   (a) Raw material conversion.
   (b) Semifinished production.
   (c) Finished production.

2.1. Raw material conversion will be a cost center that is allowed to retain a percentage of the reduction of standard costs that it manages to obtain for use in internal development and for incentives.

2.2. Production units will be profit centers, and will be allowed to retain a percentage of their profits for internal development and incentive use.

2.3. All the output units on the first level report directly
to the operations manager.

Inputs and Services

3. Inputs and services will consist of the following semiautonomous units:

(a) *Power.* The power unit will procure and distribute all the energy needs for Alpha.

(b) *Purchasing.* The purchasing unit will procure
and distribute all goods and services needed by
the Alpha operation.

(c) *Maintenance.* The maintenance unit will be responsible for large-scale renovations that require
coordination of several organizations.
Breakdown/routine maintenance will be the responsibility of maintenance services located in
other units.

(d) *Information services.* The information services
unit will collect, store, process, and disseminate
data according to the needs of user groups (accounting, payroll, recordkeeping, scheduling information, and others).

(e) *Transportation.* The transportation unit will provide the resources to meet all the transportation
needs of Alpha.
It will lease out vehicles and support systems to
other parts of the organization.

3.1. Input and service units will be profit centers that sell
their services or products to other members of the
organization at cost-plus margin.

3.2. They will be allowed to retain a percentage of their

profits for internal development and incentive uses.

3.3. They will be evaluated by the management control system on their profitability and the quality of service provided to the users.

3.4. All the input units on the first level report directly to the operations manager.

Development and Advocacy

4. Development units are responsible for change at Alpha.

4.1. Development will consist of the following units:

(a) *Engineering.* Engineering is responsible for physical and technical design and improvements at Alpha.

(b) *Industrial engineering.* Industrial engineering is responsible for efficiency improvements in the man–machine systems.

(c) *Process control engineering.* Process control engineering will be responsible for improving the quality of in-process goods.

4.2. The first level will have the following advocacy units:

(a) *Marketing.* Marketing will represent Alpha to the corporate marketing department and to customers, and will represent the needs of these groups to Alpha.

(b) *Communications.* The communications unit will represent the interest of the following parts of the external environment to Alpha and vice versa:
    (1) Government
    (2) Community

       (3) Corporation

       (4) Others as needed

4.3. In addition to their basic functions, the development and advocacy units will act as a staff function of the planning board.

4.4. These units will report directly to the operations manager.

4.5. Their services will be assigned by the operations manager.

4.6. These units will be overhead centers and receive their operation budgeting from a percentage of the operation of the whole organization.

4.7. They will be evaluated by the operations manager based on their impact on the overall performance of the Alpha operation.

Planning

5. Planning on the first level will be done by a planning board which is chaired by the operations manager.

5.1. The planning board will consist of all managers of output, input service, development and advocacy, and management control systems units who, in turn, will chair the planning boards of their units.

5.2. The planning board will be engaged in continuous interactive planning to redesign the Alpha operation as needed.

5.3. The planning board will generate policies and procedures for the Alpha system.

5.4. The planning board will state the expectations of all decisions and the real consequence and impact of those decisions will be assessed on a regular basis by the management control system.

5.5. The planning board will oversee the activities of the development and advocacy units.

5.6. The planning board will meet at least once a month.

5.7. The planning board will form and supervise the following committees and task force groups (ad hoc committees), and others as needed:

(a) Research and development.

(b) Energy.

(c) Joint labor and management safety.

(d) Facility planning.

(e) Business planning board.

(f) Training.

(g) Policy.

(h) Industrial relations.

(i) Others as the need arises.

Management Control System

6. The management control system will consist of the following semiautonomous units:

(a) *Human resources management.* The human resources management unit will monitor the internal environment in order to improve the quality of work life through regular climate surveys, will facilitate internal communications, help improve labor–management relations, help in recruiting and training, and help in career development of all personnel. (This includes facilitating internal communications, labor relations, the work climate, personnel, recruiting, training, and others.)

(b) *Output control.* Output control monitors, inspects, evaluates, and accepts or rejects materials in process or finished goods.

(c) *Financial control.* The financial control unit is responsible for the analysis of the ongoing budget and expenditure data to insure that financial regulations are adhered to.

6.1. The management control system units report to and are evaluated by the operations manager.

6.2. All units in the management control system are overhead centers that receive an operating budget taken from a percent of the total operation.

(The next section covers the "Second-Level Organization." The following is a section of the design that appears under the general heading "Environment.")

Environment

The objectives are:

1. To share resources and knowledge with the environment.
2. To promote the mutual welfare of the plants' community, employers, corporation, vendors, customers, employees and union, and of the government.
3. To maintain credibility in dealing with stakeholders.
4. To keep communication channels open with all stakeholders.

The principles of design by means of which these objectives are sought are:

1. To develop opportunity for participation and membership in community activities for all employees.

2. To provide a feedback system in order to monitor performance.

3. To not negatively affect quality of life and health of the
   community.

(Sections 7–15 are omitted.)

Customers

16. Alpha will actively seek customers with the following
    characteristics:

    (a) Financially strong.

    (b) Dynamic.

    (c) Innovative.

    (d) Noncyclical.

    (e) With growing geographic proximity.

    (f) Not price-buyers.

    16.1. Alpha customers will be identified through plant
          product sales representatives interacting with the
          controller unit, the quality assurance and quality
          control unit, corporate X products division, corpor-
          ate marketing and market research, and customers.

    16.2. Customer satisfaction will be accomplished by the
          following:

          (a) Identification of the needs of the customers
              with respect to technical assistance, product
              specification, deliveries, payment schedule,
              and new-product development.

          (b) Team visits to customer plants and customer
              visits to Greensville.

(c) Closed-loop communication systems between plant and customer to communicate the status of and the need for promised performance, through such means as encouragement of customer grading systems.

(d) Yearly customer product seminars.

16.2.1. The marketing unit will be responsible for getting the cooperation of other units necessary to accomplish the above.

16.3. There will be a quarterly training program for corporate marketing and field sales. Topics will include:

(a) Quality.

(b) Cost and profitability.

(c) Product design.

(d) Manufacturing utilization.

(e) Equipment capabilities.

(f) Deliveries and transportation.

16.3.1. These programs will last approximately one week.

16.3.2. A manual will be prepared for all employees, including plant personnel, which covers the above.

16.3.3. The marketing unit will be responsible for this training program.

16.4. The planning board will establish a semiautonomous project responsible for new product development.

16.4.1. The project will include specialists from the following areas:

(a) Engineering.

load to pick up in Chicago and deliver in New York. The company could use its own equipment to take its load to a TRANS PORT in Chicago, drop it off for continuation to Los Angeles by a hired carrier, and pick up its own load at the same place for return to New York.

6. Loading/unloading could be on/from standardized weather-proof containers that would fit on a trailer bed (as described below) and be capable of being handled by any mode of transportation.

7. Standardized containers could be owned by shippers or receivers, or be leased or rented.

8. In each city pools of bonded long-distance truck drivers would be available for hire on a short-term basis (much as Kelly Girls are currently available for secretarial assistance).

Equipment

9. In addition to one-piece trucks, and cab–trailer combinations, there would be easily assembled modular trucks consisting of five parts: (a) power packs of variable size to suit the load being carried, (b) cabs with and without sleeping accommodations for one or two people, (c) chassis to receive cabs and power packs, (d) standardized weatherproof containers of varying size that lock on, and (e) trailer beds of varying size and load-carrying capacity.

   The containers and trailer beds would be so designed that containers would easily lock on the beds and to each other to form a rigid mass.

   The modularized truck would make it possible to use a power source no larger than is required by a load, thereby conserving energy.

10. Computer programs would be available for rapidly calculating the optimal combination of modular units for any

load, destination, and delivery-time characteristics.

11. Containers would be loaded and unloaded by use of equipment much like that currently used in such loading and unloading of aircraft.

12. Trucks would be aerodynamically efficient. Air shelters between the wheels and at the back of trucks might accomplish this as well as light weight snap-on airfoils to cover loads of containers.

13. Tractors and trailers would be available with wheels for use on rail as well as on roads. These trucks would be able to move directly from one medium to the other unaided.

14. Trailers would have couplings at both ends so they could be assembled into trains pulled by either a truck tractor or a locomotive.

15. Coupled trailers would also be used in trailer trains over the road where permitted; for example, on such dedicated highways or lanes as are described below.

16. All tractors and trailers, and one-piece trucks, would have standardized towing gear at both ends to enable them to be towed or to tow any other truck.

17. Trailer beds would be so designed that they could be stacked and ride on each other, thus permitting two or three empty beds to be hauled by one tractor.

18. Tractors would be so designed that subassembly replacement would be easy, thus reducing down time for repairs. Defective subassemblies could then be repaired without immobilizing a tractor. Emphasis would be placed on designing and producing these assemblies so as to maximize their reliability and predictability; in this way, scheduled maintenance would take care of most equipment needs.

19. Intracity trucks would be equipped with radar control devices at both ends to prevent front- and rear-end collisions.

    19.1. The device at the front end would determine the

distance to the vehicle in front of the truck and, using the speed of the truck on which it is installed, would determine when its distance from the vehicle in front of it is about to become unsafe. At this point it would automatically take control of the speed of the vehicle and reduce it, signaling the driver to this effect. The driver would not be able to override this reduction.

19.2. The device at the rear end would make a similar calculation for the vehicle behind the truck. When that vehicle began to get too close, lights would blink at it, signaling the truck driver to this effect. If the vehicle behind got still closer, a sirenlike noise would be directed at the driver of the other vehicle.

20. All long-haul truck cabs would be equipped with telephones. These would operate with a headset so that the driver's hands would not be used and road noise would not be a problem. An alternative would be a soundproofed air-conditioned cab with microphone and speaker.

21. All intracity trucks would be equipped with an electronic monitoring system that would keep the driver informed about the performance of the truck in a number of ways; for example, temperature of various components (engine, tires, etc.) and gallons of fuel being consumed per mile. Audible and visible signals would indicate an approaching problem.

22. Tractors and trailers would be available for a variety of new uses. Some examples follow.

22.1. Modular factories could be mounted on trailers. These could be assembled on site to provide manufacturing facilities; for example, for manufacturing houses or parts of them. Processing units for mines could be similarly assembled.

22.2. Special-purpose classrooms (for example, labora-
tories, computing facilities, and libraries) could be
moved from school to school on different days so
that even small or remote schools could be provided
with special facilities for effective education.
Such classrooms could also be used for technical
training of industrially employed field personnel; for
example, those who repair air-conditioning systems.

22.3. Retail stores that handle specialty products normally only available in large population centers could
be made mobile. They would move between rural
and suburban shopping centers bringing big-city
shopping within reach of many.

22.4. Buses would be designed as trailers that could be
drawn by truck tractors. This would enable trucks
to haul people as well as goods. In the case of school
buses, for example, their tractors could be used for
other purposes while the people-carrying trailers
were idle. There would be audiovisual two-way
communication between the driver and passengers.
Such buses would be ideally suited for large employers who wanted to pick up and deliver their
employees rather than have them drive in individu-
ally. The savings in parking space might compen-
sate for the cost of the buses, not to mention energy
savings. The tractors could be used for work-related
activities during the day.

22.5. *Car ferries.* There would be assembly points at major
entrances and exits to limited-access highways
where automobiles headed for distant locations
could drive onto a trailer bed and be hauled to that
destination for a fee.
For example, an automobile could mount a trailer
bed in New York and be hauled to Chicago. The

driver could sleep or work in his car. Heat could be provided as it is in drive-in theaters. This would conserve energy, reduce wear and tear on drivers and their cars, and provide additional income to truckers.

22.6. Special-purpose one-piece trucks such as concrete mixers and dump and garbage trucks would be available in two pieces, tractors and trailers, so that when the trailer is not in use the tractor could be used, or when a tractor is not usable, the trailer would not have to remain idle.

Media and the Environment

23. Every city would have at least one TRANS PORT located at an easily accessible point on its periphery. TRANS PORTS would provide facilities for intermodal transfers— minimally between air, rail, and road, and where possible water and pipelines. They would provide storage facilities for goods shipped and for transportation equipment. They would include repair and maintenance services for all transportation equipment, and accommodations for their operators when they are away from home.

24. TRANS PORTS would publish schedules for LTL shipments so that shipments brought to them before a specified time would have a guaranteed delivery time at a specified destination.

25. Truck-trailers would not be permitted to operate within cities during the day (for example, from 7:00 A.M. to 11:00 P.M., Monday through Friday), but would be able to use city streets at other hours. Therefore, daytime deliveries of goods brought into the city would require transfer to smaller vehicles at TRANS PORTS. Smaller trucks used for this

purpose would be so designed as to carry the standardized containers, thus minimizing transfer time at TRANS PORTS. All modes would use the same containers to facilitate transfers between them.

26. There would be toll highways between major population centers for the exclusive use of trucks, similarly for automobiles. Truck trains would be permitted on such highways. Speed limits would be higher on these highways.

27. Truck highways could be laid on unused railroad beds.

28. On mixed-mode highways of three or more lanes, at least one lane would be reserved for trucks.
For example, on a three-lane highway the right lane would be reserved for trucks except for marked sections near entrances and exits where cars could enter these lanes. Center lanes would be for cars and truck passing. Left lanes would be reserved for car passing.

29. Dedicated truck lanes would have an electronic or magnetic guide imbedded in them so that automatic pilots in truck cabs could be used to drive the vehicle when it operates on truck-only highways or rail.

30. There would be communication-control points along main highways so that each truck could report in periodically as airplanes do to control towers. Their locations and conditions would be known at all times. These points would also provide information on road conditions and reroute trucks when necessary.

31. Truck drivers would be treated much like airline pilots. Their physical condition and working conditions would be controlled and monitored to assure their safety and that of others. There would be enforced limits on how long and how frequently they could drive. Drivers would also be subject to restrictions on the use of drugs of any kind.

Implications

There is a general theme that emerges in a qualitative way from our projections and design: cooperative, collaborative, or joint ventures. That is, most of the changes we have suggested as desirable require some acting together of a number of the relevant participants in order to bring them about. Different types of stakeholders in the trucking system must act together in order to realize the potential improvements suggested. Tractor, trailer, and container manufacturers, state and federal agencies concerned with highways, and other transportation media all have a role to play in bringing about a systematic and continuing improvement in the trucking system. Some specific recommendations along these lines follow.

1. Study of the feasibility of highways and highway lanes for the exclusive use of trucks requires collaboration with appropriate governmental agencies. Also, a similar collaboration is required in order to standardize regulations applicable to equipment and its use over all the states.

2. A joint venture with trailer and container manufacturers should be considered in order to carry forward the design and manufacture of units that can be integrated; that is, the tractor, trailer (as a "bed"), and container modules should be designed from a single point of view so as to be able to integrate them in various combinations.

3. Consideration should be given to the establishment of a pilot project with one or more railroads in order to study various ways in which an efficient rail–truck system can be realized.

4. With respect to the concept of a TRANS PORT described in our design, the development of such a facility by

means of a consortium, conceived as a profit-making
entity, should be considered.

Truck design should aim wherever possible to separation of the
tractor portion of currently "monolithic" trucks. For example,
the tractor should be made detachable from garbage trucks and
salting dump trucks so their utilization can be increased. Similarly for street-washing trucks, tank trucks, buses, vans, and so
on. In addition, consideration should be given to a truck with
only a flat bed on to which the special purpose equipment could
be mounted. Some attention should also be given to the feasibility of a front-wheel-drive tractor with retractable rear axle that
could be "bonded" with special-purpose rear ends.

To the extent that larger tractors can be justified and put into
use, the threat of foreign competition can be reduced.

Resource allocations between improvements in design and
improvements in the manufacturing process must be kept flexible so as to be able to take rapid advantage of technological
developments in energy-conserving power plants and new fuels.

SCENARIO 3

1. Mission of the Committee.

The mission of the reorganization committee is to make
recommendations concerning a new organizational structure for professional baseball that would increase the efficiency of the administration of baseball, increase the ability
of organized baseball to respond effectively to changing
social and economic conditions, and project a stronger
and more unified image of baseball.

2. Members of the Committee (omitted).

3. A Basic Structural Consideration.

> Some believe that all baseball requires is a "good sound" corporate structure and competent business management. Unfortunately, perhaps, baseball is not a business, although it obviously has its business side. It consists of twenty-six autonomous and separate businesses that cannot be subjected to a centralized management without significantly reducing that autonomy. For this reason a corporate structure cannot be imposed on baseball without changing the nature of the clubs in fundamental ways.

The composition of baseball is currently more like that of the United Nations or OPEC than that of a corporation. The ineffectiveness of these organizations derives from the same autonomous characteristics of their members as does the ineffectiveness of the current organization of baseball.

Although the model of federal government does not apply to baseball for the same reasons, it comes closer to doing so because it allows for more autonomy of the units that compose it than does a corporate structure. Therefore, we have tried to adapt this model to baseball, taking into account the fact that economics as well as politics must be considered.

Governance—that is, public management—in a democracy has three fundamental and necessarily separated but interdependent functions: the *legislative*, the *executive* (administrative), and the *judicial*.

1. The *legislative* function of baseball could be performed by a board consisting of representatives of each club. The board would also police, evaluate, and guide the executive branch.

2. The *executive* (administrative) function could be carried out by a chief executive officer (CEO) and his staff. He would be responsible for implementing the "laws" and policies set by the board, preparing and submitting plans and budgets to it for approval, and suggesting legislation.

3. The *judicial* function could be performed by a commissioner who, assisted by a small staff, would inspect, police, judge compliance with the "law," and punish those who break it.

This three-pronged concept of governance is the basis of the structural redesign of baseball shown in Figure 11.1 and described in detail in what follows.

4. The Board

Composition

4.1. The Board of Baseball shall consist of one representative designated by each club plus the chief executive officer (CEO) who shall serve as its chairman but be permitted to vote only in case of a tie.

4.2. Each club shall be permitted to designate an alternate who may attend board meetings but who shall not be permitted to speak except in the absence of the representative or unless called upon by the chairman. The alternate shall vote only when he is substituting for an absent representative.

4.3. No others will be permitted to attend board meetings except when requested by the chairman to report to the board.

4.4. By a simple majority vote the board may go into executive session from which all but representatives,

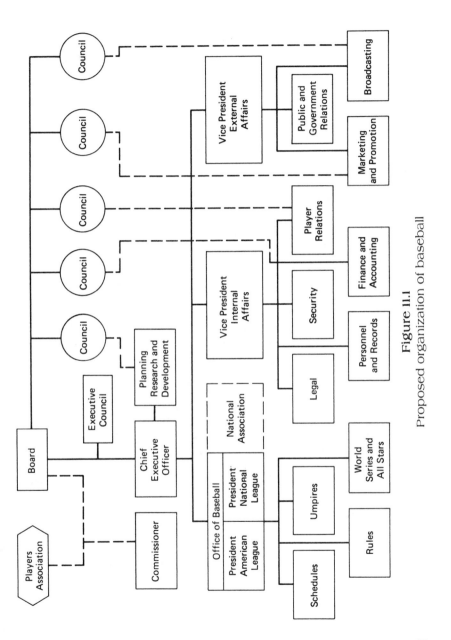

Figure 11.1
Proposed organization of baseball

147

alternates substituting for them, and the chairman shall be excluded.

Meetings

4.5. The board shall hold regular meetings once each quarter at regularly scheduled times.

4.6. Agenda of board meetings shall be set by the executive council and distributed to board members and their alternates, along with supporting documents, no less than two weeks before each meeting.

Voting

4.7. Each vote from the American League shall carry a weight of one (1). Each vote from the National League shall carry a weight of fourteen-twelfths (14/12), so that the total weighted vote from each league shall be equal. (If the number of teams in a league changes, appropriate adjustments will be made to preserve this equality.)

4.8. All motions, with the exception of *reserve motions* identified in the next section, shall be passed upon the simple majority of weighted affirmative votes. (At present, with 12 teams in one league and 14 in the other, this means a weighted affirmative vote of 15 or more is required to pass a motion.)

4.9. Reserve motions are those motions that affect or bear on the following issues:

(*a*) Designated-hitter rules.

(*b*) League expansion.

(*c*) Transfer of franchise.

(*d*) Three-divisional play.

(e) Inter-league play.

In order for a reserve motion to pass, a majority of affirmative votes in each league is required.

4.10. Issues may be added to or subtracted from this list by a majority vote in each league.

Functions

4.11. The board shall legislate for the conduct and operation of baseball and will establish its constitution which it will modify when necessary. (Legislation shall include taxation of clubs.)

4.12. The board shall formulate and police a code of ethics for club management.

4.13. The board shall select the CEO.

4.14. The board shall participate in the selection of a commissioner as described below.

4.15. The CEO's appointment of a vice president requires the ratification of the board.

4.16. The CEO's plans and proposed budget shall be brought to the board for approval, rejection, or modification.

4.17. The board shall, in collaboration with the CEO, develop an orientation program for new owners.

4.18. The board shall produce minutes of its meetings and arrange for distribution within two weeks after its meeting to board members and their alternates.

4.19. The board shall maintain a permanent record of all its business, including the details of all votes, an indexed set of minutes, and matters the executive committee has taken up on behalf of the board.

(In all other respects, the board shall operate as it does now.)

5.   The Executive Council

Composition

5.1.   This council shall be composed of six representatives on the board (three from each league), the CEO who shall serve as chairman but be permitted to vote only in the case of a tie, and the two league presidents as nonvoting members.

5.2.   Club representatives who serve on the council shall have three-year terms, two (one from each league) being replaced each year. No club shall succeed itself on the council.

Meetings

5.3.   The council shall have at least one regularly scheduled meeting between each regular board meeting, and shall have additional meetings as required. Additional meetings may be called either by any two council members or by the CEO.

Voting

5.4.   All voting shall be by simple majority, the chairman breaking ties.

Functions

5.5.   The council shall interpret the laws and policies of the board and advise the CEO in this regard.

5.6.   The council shall set the agenda for board meetings and be responsible for its distribution at least two weeks in advance of these meetings.

5.7. The council shall review biannually the activities and operations of the executive function and report its findings to the board.

5.8. The council shall present issues and recommendations to the board.

5.9. The council shall produce minutes of its meetings and arrange for their distribution within one week of its meetings to board members and their alternates.

5.10. Within a few days after each of its meetings each club representative who is a council member shall telephone three or four designated board members not on the council to report on the meeting.

6. The Office of Baseball

6.1. All offices of baseball shall be consolidated in one location with an appropriate reduction of overlapping of staff personnel.

7. The Chief Executive Officer (CEO)

7.1. The CEO shall relate to the board and his subordinates in the same way that corporate CEOs relate to their boards and subordinates.

7.2. The CEO shall be selected by the board for a five-year (renewable) term. (He should have skill and experience in business management and a great knowledge of and interest in baseball.)

7.3. The CEO shall nominate those to fill vice presidencies and submit his nominations to the board for ratification.

7.4. The CEO shall have overall responsibility for the administration of baseball, and for submitting annual plans and budgets to the board.

8. The Planning, Research, and Development Unit

8.1. This unit shall have a director and a small staff part of whom shall be appropriate professionals.

8.2. The unit will be responsible for preparing developmental plans for baseball and for conducting the research necessary for preparing these plans, as required by the CEO, the vice presidents, the councils, and department heads in the execution of their responsibilities.

8.3. If the workload of this unit exceeds its capacity, it will contract for additional professional services from appropriate external sources.

9. The Vice Presidents

9.1 There shall be two vice presidents, one for internal affairs and one for external affairs.

9.2. They will serve five-year terms (renewable) congruent with the term of the CEO.

9.3. The vice presidents shall be responsible for the operations of the departments reporting to them. (See Figure 11.1.) They will also be responsible for selecting the directors of these departments, subject to the approval of the CEO.

10. The Commissioner

10.1. The commissioner shall serve a five-year renewable term.

10.2. He shall be a person with experience in the public justice system.

10.3. He shall be selected in the following way:

(a) The board shall nominate at least two candidates for the position, except where reappointment is involved.

(b) The Players' Association shall select one of these candidates or reject all.

(c) In case of rejection, a new set of nominations shall be prepared by the board.

(d) This process shall continue until a choice is made.

(e) The process shall begin no less than one year before the end of the incumbent's term to allow sufficient time for the process.

10.4 The commissioner shall be augmented by a small staff.

10.5. He shall have all the functions of a judicial system: policing, judging, and issuing punishment.

10.6. He shall be empowered to levy fines up to a specified amount.

10.7. The only appeal of his decisions shall be to the public courts.

11. The League Presidents

11.1. League presidents shall be selected by their respective leagues for a five-year (renewable) term.

11.2. They will serve as co-directors of an office of base-ball that has the four functions shown in Figure 11.1. If they cannot reach agreement, the CEO shall settle the issue.

11.3. They shall serve as nonvoting members of the executive council, and as voting members of (a) the planning, research, and development unit and (b) the players' relations council, and such other councils as the board may determine.

12. The Councils

12.1. In addition to the executive council, there shall be five others:

(a) Player relations.
(b) Finance and accounting.
(c) Marketing and promotions.
(d) Broadcasting.
(e) Planning, research, and development.

12.2. Each of these councils shall include:

(a) At least one member of the executive council.
(b) At least three other board members chosen so that with the member of the executive council, there will be an equal number from each league.
(c) Other club officials or appropriate professionals selected by the board.
(d) The CEO, who shall also serve as the chairman of the planning, research, and development council, which council shall also include the league presidents as members.

(e) The appropriate vice president, who shall serve as chairman except in the case of the planning, research, and development council.

12.3. Minutes of the council meetings will be distributed to all nonparticipating members of the board and their alternates within a week after the meeting.

(In all other respects the councils shall perform as now.)

13. The Departments (omitted)

14. The National Association (omitted)

Postscript: Player–Owner Relations

Major league baseball is currently torn by conflict between club owners and the players as represented by the Players' Association and their agents. In such a situation it is natural for each of the parties to try to increase their strength, their ability to "win" encounters. Such increases, however, invariably escalate the conflict and increase the cost of winning as well as losing. As in war, the more equal the power of the adversaries, the more protracted and damaging is their conflict.

The only way to eliminate such conflict is by eliminating it— converting it to collaboration.

The adversaries in baseball obviously have a number of common objectives, including their commitment to the game and the fans. They can benefit, therefore, from cooperation with each other. This is not only desirable, but possible. Labor–management cooperation has been growing like a tidal wave in industrial circles. Under the name of "quality of work life" such efforts have resulted in dramatic increases in productivity, quality of product, and, perhaps most important, satisfaction derived from work. Absenteeism, sabotage, lateness, and accidents have been significantly reduced.

For these reasons it is recommended that the Board of Baseball initiate an effort to establish player–owner collaboration.

There is virtually nothing to lose by the failure of such an effort, but a great deal to gain if it succeeds.

REFERENCES

■ ■ ■

Ackoff, R. L., *The Art of Problem Solving*, John Wiley & Sons, New York, 1978.

Ackoff, R. L., *Creating the Corporate Future*, John Wiley & Sons, New York, 1981.

Ackoff, R. L., and Elsa Vergara, "Creativity in Problem Solving and Planning: A Review," *European Journal of Operational Research*, **7** (1981), 1–13.

Bierman, H., C. Bonini, and W. Hausman, *Quantitative Analysis for Business Decisions*, Richard D. Irwin, Homewood, Ill., 1981.

Campbell, D., and J. Stanley, *Experimental and Quasi-Experimental Design for Research*, Houghton Mifflin, Boston, 1966.

Hillier, F., and G. Lieberman, *Introduction to Operations Research*, Holden Day, San Francisco, 1980.

McFarlan, F. W., and J. J. McKenney, *Corporate Information Systems Management: The Issues Facing Senior Executives*, Dow Jones-Irwin, Homewood, Ill., 1982.

Mendenhall, W., *Introduction to Linear Models and the Design and Analysis of Experiments*, Duxbury Press, Boston, 1968.

Sagasti, F., and R. L. Ackoff, "Possible and Likely Futures of Urban Transportation," *Socio-Economic Planning Science*, **5** (1971), 413–428.

Index